Assessment of the Exceptional Learner in the Regular Classroom

Assessment of the Exceptional Learner in the Regular Classroom

Mary Ross Moran
University of Kansas

LOVE PUBLISHING COMPANY
Denver, Colorado 80222

Copyright © 1978 Love Publishing Company
Printed in the U.S.A.
ISBN 0-89108-077-5
Library of Congress Catalog Card Number 78-50501

Contents

Introduction

Numerous guidelines to direct assessment of the exceptional child in a special services program are available to the special educator. However, limited direction has been offered to the classroom teacher who bears responsibility for initial identification, academic diagnosis, and appropriate referral of learners who present evidence of a handicapping condition. The primary purpose of this book is to offer the regular classroom teacher specific guidelines for the many decisions he or she must make in assessing mildly handicapped children in the classroom, determining whether referral is indicated, identifying appropriate referral sources, and interpreting reports of testing by other professionals. This book focuses on initial assessment, or diagnosis, preparatory to designing and implementing an individualized education program (IEP). Discussion of the steps involved in the writing, implementation, and continuous monitoring of the education plan is beyond the scope of this book.

Legislation governing the education of exceptional learners, especially the Education for All Handicapped Children Act of 1975, and interpretations of the "least restrictive environment" have placed more and more mildly handicapped children in the regular program as previously unserved severely handicapped learners enter public school special education programs. Mildly handicapped students in regular classrooms constitute three distinct groups, each of which places different demands upon the regular classroom teacher.

1. One group is identified, referred for evaluation, and assigned to receive regularly scheduled services on an ongoing basis from a resource-room teacher, reading teacher, or itinerant special tutor while remaining in the regular classroom for most of the day. For this group, the assessment role of the regular classroom teacher is limited. His or her initial identification of a pupil considered to be at risk for academic failure is followed by academic testing in the classroom and formulation of questions which cannot be answered by means of classroom procedures. These referral questions are forwarded to ancillary personnel such as school psychologists or special educators who are responsible for employing appropriate assessment procedures to answer the presenting problems. When the resolution of a pupil's academic problems takes the form of a recommendation for placement in special services for part of the day, the burden of assessment of that pupil is shared with the special services personnel who schedule regular reevaluation and review to guide decisions about termination or continuation of services. The role of the regular classroom teacher shifts to maintaining continuity of instructional, grading, and behavior management practices between the special and regular programs, along with providing data on instructional outcomes to special services personnel engaged in formative evaluation.
2. A second group of exceptional learners in the regular classroom is identified, referred to ancillary personnel

for evaluation, and assigned by the evaluators to the regular classroom teacher who is to implement a program designed by specialists. For this group, the teacher bears the responsibility for initial identification, academic testing in the classroom, and formulation of referral questions just as for the first group. In addition, however, the teacher who is to implement the recommendations of support personnel in the classroom carries the responsibility for interpreting the information, inferences, and judgments presented in a report and translating them into classroom practices. The assessment role changes to that of monitoring progress, or *formative evaluation*, which is an ongoing responsibility of the classroom teacher. Referral for reevaluation should not be part of the teacher's role, since a regular schedule for review should be incorporated into the individualized education plan designed by the special services personnel.

3. A third group is identified by the regular classroom teacher as at risk for academic failure, tested in the classroom by the teacher, and instructed exclusively by the classroom teacher whose assistance from support personnel may be limited to consultation on methods and materials. While accountability for the first two groups can be shared with fellow professionals, the responsibility for the third group is assumed by the classroom teacher alone. He or she undertakes identification of the problems, diagnosis of academic status, planning for and delivery of instructional modifications to meet individual needs, and evaluation of outcomes. This group constitutes the major challenge to the regular classroom teacher, as it includes the borderline learners who could be overlooked because their handicapping condition is neither obvious nor severe.

The teacher's potential for effective participation in assessment of these groups for purposes of preparing the IEP has not been realized, due to several factors. First, the training of regular

9

elementary and secondary classroom teachers has not provided them with a systematic, practical approach to identification, diagnostic assessment, referral, and interpretation of test results for exceptional learners. Second, teachers have been led to feel inadequate to assess special learners because of the proliferation and increasing sophistication of formal testing instruments. Third, teachers have been placed in awe of credential-laden specialists such as the school psychologist, the learning disabilities teacher, the counselor, the psychometrist, and the methods and materials consultant. Fourth, regular classroom teachers have not profited from the current plentiful supply of teachers in terms of a decrease in class size; instead, most elementary teachers remain responsible for 25 to 30 learners, and secondary teachers see 150 to 180 students per day.

For these reasons, classroom teachers have not rushed forward to assume an expanded role in assessment of the mildly handicapped student in the regular classroom who requires an IEP. But it is a great loss to the diagnostic-remedial process if the teacher is not an active participant in the systematic investigation of solutions to instructional problems presented by handicapping conditions. Since the success of the program for the mainstreamed exceptional learner ultimately rests with the regular classroom teacher who is responsible for most of the direct instruction, there are compelling reasons to utilize the unique skills of the teacher at the earliest stages of the diagnostic-remedial continuum.

This book represents an attempt to organize the teacher's task so he or she can assume a major role in diagnostic assessment of the exceptional learner in the regular classroom. Because the identification of a handicapped student ideally should occur early in the learner's progress through school, the emphasis of the book and most of its examples are directed toward the elementary teacher. However, the procedures described for identification, diagnosis, referral, and team participation apply equally to the secondary teacher whose class load includes mainstreamed exceptional learners, some of whom may not have been identified at the elementary level.

Part I-Identification presents criteria for determining when a pupil can be considered at risk for academic failure. What information is already available in school records to identify such learners? What is the practical way to identify behaviors which constitute academic deficits or which interfere with learning? What is the teacher's role in screening pupils to identify possible handicapping conditions?

Part II-Diagnosis presents methods of using informal tests, instructional materials, and systematic observation to gain precise information about academic skills preparatory to referral or classroom intervention. Does a teacher have a role in determining perceptual or intellectual functioning, or social-emotional status? How can a teacher schedule time in a school day to test academic strengths and weaknesses? What testing resources are available to the teacher?

Part III-Referral includes criteria for determining whether, and to whom, a pupil should be referred, the levels of data to be gained from formal evaluation, and considerations of referral practices which can lead to useful test results. How does a teacher determine a need for assistance from other professional personnel? How can the teacher communicate what he or she already knows about the pupil? What can be done to prepare the pupil for evaluation?

Part IV-The Assessment Team outlines approaches to analyzing reports of testing by other professionals, and offers suggestions for effective relationships with members of the diagnostic team. What are the types of statements to be found in reports? What can be done if reported statements do not agree with the teacher's view of the pupil? What is the teacher's role in the ongoing professional contacts with support personnel?

1

Identification

With the exception of a few learners scheduled to receive special services continued from the previous year, the students assigned to a given teacher at the beginning of the school term must be presumed by that teacher to be his or her total responsibility. This is, however, a rebuttable presumption. Evidence may accumulate to indicate that the teacher should enlist the assistance of support personnel to determine whether a given student demonstrates a handicapping condition. However, such a question cannot be presented to a fellow professional until the teacher has made the initial identification of a pupil who requires closer investigation.

Some school districts may require a classroom teacher to undertake specific screening procedures designed to identify students for possible referral. But the rationale for such procedures may be difficult to formulate, and the ethical question of subjecting all students to what could be construed as unnecessary testing may render such a course unjustifiable. Instead, it seems reasonable to assume that students with possible handicapping conditions can be separated for purposes of referral, diagnostic testing, and individualized programming by systematic attention to readily accessible information over the first few weeks of the school term.

AVAILABLE IDENTIFICATION DATA

Incidental Observation

To begin to arrive at an initial identification of pupils who may be at risk for academic failure, the teacher should make use of readily available information. From the first day, he or she can gather informal impressions. These impressions can be categorized by dividing the class according to two preliminary questions: Which students demonstrate age-appropriate and grade-level academic behaviors within the normal range for students in this classroom? Which pupils stand out in some way as exhibiting unusual academic behaviors? These questions lead to the formation of two groups of learners in the classroom, and they focus on academic behaviors only.

At the Identification stage, the teacher should focus solely on academic behaviors for two reasons. First, the range of possible behaviors to be exhibited in a classroom is so great that the teacher could easily be distracted from his or her primary responsibilities by trying to assess characteristics which are either irrelevant to the academic process or are beyond a teacher's competence to judge. The teacher is trained to observe task behaviors within a given domain, and by limiting the observations initially to that domain, he or she is in the best position to make use of those skills. A student may indeed have nonacademic behavior problems, or health problems, and the teacher is not insensitive to such concerns. However, *the teacher's first responsibility is to be alert to response to instruction.*

The second reason for focusing solely on academic behaviors is that if language, perceptual, motor, social, or emotional problems of a given student are serious enough to warrant intervention, they are sure to be manifested in failure to respond to instruction, and thus it is more likely that they will be identified if the focus is on academic performance. If such problems do not inhibit academic growth, there may be no justification for action by the teacher. Probably, many children compensate for a variety of handicaps and function academically up to their potential despite some variation from accepted developmental norms.

Thus, at the Identification stage, the teacher should attempt no more than a simple dichotomy. In the first group will be those students whose academic performance is unremarkable. In the second group will be those who exhibit behaviors which set them apart in some way when their academic performance is compared with that of the typical learner at that level. Although the focus of this book is handicapped learners, those who demonstrate unusual abilities such as insightful questions or comments, production of an unusual volume or quality of work, creative approaches to problem-solving, or talent in art or music should also be considered for a closer look.

To be effective as an initial screening approach, this dichotomy must be taken literally. Every learner who stands out academically from the typical students of the teacher's experience with a given grade level must be considered for further assessment.

In drawing this dichotomy, a teacher is wise to base decisions on his or her own incidental impressions of the students, rather than basing the decisions on prior information about the learners. If the teacher was in the same building last year, some information about non-achieving students or behavior problems is probably known, but such information is best ignored. The student deserves to be met from an unbiased point of view, since he or she may behave quite differently after maturing over the summer, and in interaction with a different teacher's personality. The teacher would also be wise to forego expectations based on experiences with older brothers and sisters. Jim Jones may have been a model student; Sally Jones may demonstrate a serious disability. Jack Smith may have been a nonachieving behavior problem; Nancy Smith may be a highly motivated, successful student.

Nor should the teacher be concerned at the Identification stage with possible *reasons* for failure to respond to academic instruction. That question is reserved for the assessment team. At this point, the teacher's task is to draw a gross distinction between those students who respond appropriately to instruction and those whose response sets them apart as varying from the typical performance.

During this incidental observation, the teacher is to be alert to questionable behavior of individual students: one who does not complete a reasonable quantity of work within the time allotted for independent work; one who does not follow directions, resulting in work prepared inaccurately or at variance with verbal or written instructions; one who requests frequent teacher aid (e.g., not beginning work upon oral directions but waiting for the teacher to demonstrate the task); one who reads orally with many word-recognition errors or demonstrates poor comprehension of what was read; one whose approach to tasks is exceptionally slow, purposeless, or disorganized; one who frequently cannot locate the place in the text, loses work papers, or does not move to the proper location with the group during instruction; one who demonstrates a tremor when holding a pencil; one who stares into space, engages in repetitive motor activity, or exhibits other competing activity during independent work periods; one who reacts with crying or a tantrum when a task becomes frustrating; one whose language or speech gives the impression of a chronologically younger child; one who seems to master a concept today but forgets it tomorrow; one who must be given a number of trials to complete a task. Of course, this list is not exhaustive. There are as many types of academic behaviors as there are learners in a room. It is the atypical or broad extreme of behavior which should attract the teacher's attention.

After the dichotomy is drawn on the basis of incidental impressions during the usual classroom routine (which should be accomplished within the first few weeks of the school year), the teacher is in a position to make use of other available data to confirm or disconfirm impressions about academic status. For those pupils who are placed in the risk group—certainly no more than 10 to 12 in a class of 30—additional information must be sought.

School Records

The first source of additional information is the school cumulative record card or record file. If data are summarized on a single card, the card usually shows the birthdate, date of school entry, previous schools attended, names of previous teachers in the same building, attendance record, and grades for each subject for each year of attendance. If group measures of intellectual functioning have been administered, the card also shows an IQ which may be in terms of full scale, verbal, and performance quotients. On the back of the card may be printouts from testing services, showing the percentiles on group achievement tests. Some cards allow room for brief anecdotal comments by teachers. In file folders, data may be more comprehensive. Individual grade cards, original test booklets for some tests, and more detailed comments by teachers may be included, along with reports of any psycho-eductional evaluations which may have been conducted.

The first step is to determine any record of a student in the risk group having been referred for evaluation by a previous teacher or perhaps assigned to special services in the past. Although the teacher should have been advised if a student in the class is scheduled for special services evaluation or is presently on a caseload list, sometimes such information is not conveyed promptly at the beginning of the year.

The second step is to determine the pattern of grades in prior years. It is essential to establish the time of onset of academic problems. If the record indicates that below-average grades began in first grade and continued to the present, the question of developmental disabilities may be raised. If, instead, the student earned average grades in early years but demonstrated a reversal in the intermediate grades, a situational disturbance or emotional

17

problems manifested in low achievement would be more likely than would retardation or learning disability. Neither the teacher nor anyone else is competent to make a differential diagnosis on the basis of records of grades, but the information is helpful in planning the diagnostic testing which is to follow, and in formulating referral questions.

The third inspection should be a comparison of the pattern of grades with the attendance record. The record should be checked for length of absences, time of year when they occurred, and the grades which followed each period of absence. If lengthy absences occurred in first or second grade, inadequate continuity of instruction in basic skills is as suspect as is any handicapping condition to explain academic problems. Periods of frequent absences over several years suggest serious health or family problems, while absence only during the winter months may indicate chronic upper respiratory infections warranting investigation of possible hearing loss and language retardation. Inspection of the absence record may reveal that low grades occurred only after periods of frequent or lengthy absence, or that a student missed enough instruction in early years to account for failure to master basic academic skills. This information is critical when questions of referral or diagnostic testing arise later in the procedures.

The fourth source of information in the record is the number of schools the pupil has attended. In a mobile society, it is not unusual to find that a fifth-grade student may have attended four different schools. The learner may have been exposed to a phonics-oriented basal reader and a traditional mathematics curriculum in one school; to a linguistic reading series and new math in another. The results of frequent moves are similar to those of chronic absence, in that continuity of instruction is disrupted.

The printouts provided by test scoring services should be consulted next to determine whether test results correspond to classroom performance. If at all possible, the standardized test results should be investigated beyond the global percentile rank or grade-equivalent score. Such data are not well enough refined to yield useful information about students who are not performing appropriately in the classroom. Instead, the teacher should attempt to gain access to the test booklet completed by the pupil. Examination of response patterns can reveal whether the learner might have misunderstood test directions, missed relatively easy items while answering more difficult ones correctly, made systematic errors or random mistakes, or lost points by completing only half the items.

Such information places the global score or percentile rank into perspective, and it offers clues about the conditions under which diagnostic testing in the classroom must take place. If allowing additional time to the student or presenting a visual model of a marking system instead of verbal directions is suggested by the pattern of responses on a group test, the teacher has gained valuable information. In the absence of the test booklet completed by the student, a blank booklet can reveal the demands placed upon the pupil, and the computer printout will show relative strengths and weaknesses within the content sampled by the test.

After all of the above information has been drawn from the cumulative record, a teacher may wish to check the performance of the pupil against the IQ recorded on the card. If a group measure has been administered in the classroom, the IQ may not represent the optimal performance of the pupil who is a nonachiever. Therefore, the IQ from a group test should be considered the low end of the possible range of intellectual functioning level for a low-achieving child, especially one who is experiencing reading difficulties.

If the group IQ is considered as only an estimate of the range within which the pupil is functioning, it can provide a limited frame of reference to reveal gross discrepancies. For example, a student who scored in the superior range on the group IQ test who is performing well above grade level in the classroom should be considered for referral to a program for the gifted. A student with a high IQ who is performing below grade level in one or more skills areas may be demonstrating the effects of a learning disability or emotional disturbance. The student who is performing at a low level in the classroom but also yielded a below-average IQ may be a slow learner or a retarded pupil working up to capacity. A check of the group IQ against classroom performance will not and should not classify a student in the teacher's frame of reference; however, this information should be added to other information to provide further data for diagnostic testing or referral.

Another piece of information which may be available in the cumulative record is anecdotal comments by previous teachers. Although such comments, if consulted without purpose, can bias a teacher, they can also serve to alert one to characteristics of the student which should be taken into account in referral or diagnostic testing. For example, if a learner is said to be typically disorganized in approaching tasks, motorically very active and aggressive toward other pupils on the playground, this information would be helpful in planning the amount of structure to be placed upon the student.

Whether it is part of the office file or available through the nurse's office, the health record should also be inspected to determine whether a hearing evaluation has been recommended following a sweep check, whether the pupil has passed vision screenings, and whether any chronic illnesses are recorded. The nurse may also know if any medications are administered at home before the pupil comes to school. The record may show that the student once wore glasses, although the teacher notes that he or she is not now wearing them. Indications that vision or hearing should be evaluated clinically are frequently uncovered by checking the health record.

While most teachers recognize the value of checking hearing and vision screenings, sometimes they fail to see the relevance of the educational history. Certainly the history is not to be equated with current information, but it provides the context in which to evaluate current information. Decisions made without reference to history can be costly in terms of lost time and overlooked clues. For example, if two pupils fail to follow verbal directions in the classroom, decisions would be quite different for a student who has a history of chronic absence in the winter months through the primary grades and depressed verbal scores on a group IQ, and for another pupil with similar performance and verbal scores whose attendance record and grades were average until this year. The first student is a candidate for referral for an audiological and language evaluation; the second may respond to classroom intervention since the problem appears to be behavioral or situational.

Work Products

The third source of available information is the daily work products of the student. Although a detailed analysis of work products is appropriately called diagnosis rather than identification, certain aspects of the learner's characteristics become apparent upon cursory examination of work products.

Fine-motor skills such as copying letters or numerals, drawing figures for an art project, arranging materials for a science exhibit, or organizing puzzle parts can be assessed from work products. Written work which is characterized by poorly formed letters, reversals, or disproportionate spatial relationships is easily discovered, but reliability of these features over a few weeks' time should be sought since almost all young learners reverse some letters, and inaccurately formed letters can result from haste or carelessness as well as from developmental lag in motor skills.

Worksheets can be examined to determine whether a student proceeded as directed or completed a page incorrectly due to failure to follow directions. For example, if the pupil underlined the consonant heard at the end of the word instead of the one at the beginning of the word, as the teacher instructed, such a pattern could be verified on other products to determine the extent of inattention to directions.

The quantity of work produced in a given time is also of interest if it differs from that of the typical learner. Work products can reveal whether the student's approach to tasks is disorganized, incomplete, prone to careless errors. Products can disclose sequencing problems such as transposition of letters in words or of words in sentences. Thus, if examination of work products goes beyond a mere determination of a correct or incorrect response, a great deal of preliminary information about a student's academic status can be gained by even a superficial evaluation of work products.

PRIORITIES FOR ACADEMIC DIAGNOSIS

At the Identification stage, the classroom teacher is to take advantage of information available through normal daily interaction with and observation of learners, through reference to pupil records, and through examination of routine work products. At this stage the teacher does not need to spend extra time to derive information. He or she designs no special diagnostic or intervention techniques and does not depart from the instructional role to assume the role of diagnostician.

This stage differs from the following (diagnosis) stage in that identification is based upon readily available information, while diagnosis is based upon information yielded by special testing or intervention procedures undertaken by the teacher. *The Identification stage results in the division of students according to a simple dichotomy—one group of learners who are responding appropriately to instruction and a second group of learners who are not responding appropriately to instruction and are considered at risk for academic failure.*

The risk group may be further subdivided by examining available data. Some few pupils—those already on caseload lists or scheduled to receive services—need not be considered for diagnosis or referral. Another small group of pupils, who may fall into the risk group on the basis of a few behaviors which set them apart, may be considered by the teacher to exhibit such minor deviations that they might be expected to function within the broad range of average for the class. Still others may be determined to be lacking in mastery of specific skills for reasons readily identifiable by examination of the school history, such as problems attendant upon switching from initial teaching alphabet to traditional orthography, or adjusting to the third school in four years.

Those in the risk group can thus be refined to two subgroups: students whose academic problems can be accounted for by conditions external to the learner; and students who may manifest handicapping conditions. The second subgroup will have the higher priority for immediate diagnosis, since they will need to be referred to support personnel for diagnostic workups in addition to the academic evaluation conducted by the teacher. Because the referral process may involve waiting for open appointments with school psychologists or community resources such as physical therapists or pediatricians, students who appear at the Identification stage to exhibit possible handicaps should be at the top of the list for academic assessment by the teacher.

Certainly, students whose academic problems result from situational factors require special provisions also, but the solution to their problems tends to involve accelerated developmental instruction rather than modifications of procedures or materials which may be required for a handicapped pupil. Therefore, the teacher probably has enough information at the Identification stage to begin to program adequately for the student who is shifting from initial teaching alphabet to traditional orthography or for the pupil who didn't have a consistent phonics program as a result of missing too much instruction. Of course, a given student may be demonstrating in academic performance the result of both situational factors (such as inadequate or inconsistent instruction) and a handicapping condition, so the two are not mutually exclusive. Therefore, if a student who appeared to be having academic problems due to situational factors does not respond to developmental instruction, this student might become a candidate for intensive diagnosis or referral at a later date.

2

Diagnosis

When a student has been identified as at risk for academic failure and as exhibiting a possible handicapping condition, the next step is to quantify and describe those specific characteristics which warrant further investigation. Determination of a cause for concern is not enough. The nature of the concern and the extent of the problem must be ascertained prior to referral or classroom intervention. The teacher must subject the identified learners to a systematic appraisal which will result in precise description of academic strengths and weaknesses and task behaviors.

' Diagnostic evaluation for purposes of planning an educational program is not an either-or consideration. It is, rather, a matter of degree. To what extent must any given student be evaluated in order to yield sufficient information to guide formation of a plan? Every exceptional youngster, regardless of the category of exceptionality into which he or she appears to fit, is an individual with different needs in terms of a program and, therefore, different needs in regard to diagnosis. No single battery of tests, however comprehensive, will serve the diagnostic needs of every exceptional learner; nor will every exceptional student need a comprehensive battery of tests.

Many types of evaluation can take place—assessment of achievement, health status, muscle coordination, social interaction, self esteem, problem-solving approaches, coping behaviors, self-care skills, and conceptualization of experience—to name just a few. Also, different levels of evaluation might be undertaken, such as the Academic Functioning Level, Process Functioning Level, and Cognitive/Affective Functioning Level (all described in Part III as one way of organizing the referral decisions to be made by the teacher). A regular classroom teacher must cut across all these possibilities to examine the teacher's appropriate role in the diagnostic process.

RATIONALE FOR TEACHER DIAGNOSIS

In undertaking the diagnostic role in the classroom, the teacher does not usurp the function of other specialists. It is not the teacher's job to estimate levels of motor or perceptual functioning, intellectual functioning, or social-emotional status. If information gathered during the Identification stage has led to questions about the student's functioning in these areas, such concerns are appropriately formulated into referral questions and forwarded to support personnel along with the results of the teacher's own academic testing. *To make diagnostic statements about the student's status in regard to motor, perceptual, intellectual, social or emotional status is beyond the assessment role of the regular classroom teacher.*

Instead, the function of the classroom teacher is to render a precise description of behavior in his or her own area of expertise—academic skills. This description has value in its own right. It should never be seen as a substitute for a more comprehensive set of procedures which might be undertaken by a team of experts or as a temporary measure until the pupil can be seen by specialists. The teacher *is* a specialist and, within the academic area of expertise, the best qualified to evaluate the student's status. Therefore, the academic evaluation undertaken by the teacher is to take place regardless of the probability that a given learner will be referred to support personnel for further diagnosis. The teacher should take responsibility for establishing precise levels of skills in reading, mathematics, spelling, and writing, and for determining entry levels for instruction in basic subject matter areas within the classroom curriculum.

Because academic assessment in the classroom is a time-consuming undertaking which is superimposed upon the regular instructional duties, a classroom teacher must be convinced of the rationale for accepting this responsibility. Arguments in favor of teacher assessment of academic skills are plentiful. First, the teacher is familiar with the classroom materials and the demands which will be placed upon the pupil. The teacher is in the best position to judge which skills are essential for progress through, say, the fifth grade. Second, the teacher has access to almost unlimited samples of the learner's task behavior and need not base decisions upon a two-hour observation. Third, because the teacher sees the learner at various times of the day and over many days, the assessment is likely to be more reliable than that of a psychometrist who must judge whether he or she has seen the learner's optimal performance. Fourth, the teacher has an opportunity to collect observational data from independent seatwork, response to group instruction, and trial teaching— procedures which are not available to the psychometrist but which represent the terminal behavior in a classroom.

Even though they are capable of precise academic evaluation and may be willing to do it, many teachers may hesitate to undertake the task because they believe that: (a) they must administer and interpret formal, standardized tests; (b) they must have specialized knowledge of test construction to develop their own tests; (c) precise testing takes too much time; and (d) neither the available time nor adequate conditions for testing exist in the regular classroom. These are valid concerns, and they deserve discussion.

RESOURCES FOR TEACHER DIAGNOSIS

Formal, Standardized Tests

At the outset, it must be pointed out that formal standardized tests of academic achievement developed from two needs which are not major concerns of the classroom teacher. The first reason for such tests is to enable administrators and subject matter specialists responsible for overall curriculum to judge how students in a given district or area compare with a normative sample nationwide; this need not concern a teacher whose immediate responsibility is to describe the reading and math skills of John Jones in order to design a program for him. The second reason for formal tests is that they provide a shortcut means to enable a few items to predict performance on many items; since the teacher has access to many samples of behavior, such a shortcut is unnecessary.

Standardized, norm-referenced tests are designed to provide variability and to discriminate between pupils. Items for the final version of a formal test are not selected because they represent the most essential content, but rather on the basis of their ability to elicit differential responses, so that if too many students pass an item or too many fail it, it is not an acceptable item. Such sampling techniques are of limited interest to a teacher who must decide on the basis of skills which arithmetic text to place in John's hands on Monday morning.

The value of formal, standardized testing over other types of systematic observation is that placing each testee under similar conditions demanding the same tasks allows a teacher to perceive minor differences which might not be otherwise apparent. For example, if the teacher is administering a standardized, norm-referenced group test, he or she can observe the group and note readily which students: (a) do not begin promptly; (b) watch other students for cues to test behavior; (c) proceed bottom to top, right to left, or in some other atypical fashion across test pages; (d) use compensating devices such as finger counting during an arithmetic test; (e) fail to follow directions (such as circling instead of underlining); (f) do not complete the task because of distractibility or daydreaming.

This type of observation is useful in describing the performance of individual pupils, since standardized conditions make unusual task behaviors stand out. The teacher's role in administering such group achievement tests is not in question. As long as standardized administration procedures are followed, timing is accurate, group size is manageable, and conditions are as favorable as possible, the teacher need have no concern about administering standardized tests to the entire class.

With the development of *individual* standardized formal instruments to determine achievement levels of pupils who may require individualized programs, the question of who is to undertake such testing has arisen. Consideration of the relative strengths and weaknesses of specific standardized individual tests of achievement or the training which must precede such testing is beyond the scope of this discussion. Instead, the relevant question is whether the regular classroom teacher should be expected or permitted to administer such tests.

In some cases, guidelines for state funding of special services specify that certain individual achievement tests must be administered, but the guidelines do not state that only certified school psychologists may administer them; indeed, the publishers of many such tests advertise that classroom teachers may administer them. But should they do so? The question must be answered according to local philosophy and standards. However, some considerations would argue against the use of formal, standardized individual achievement tests by teachers. Two of those arguments are based upon disadvantages of formal, standardized test instruments in revealing a student's precise academic skills; two other considerations are based upon differences between a teacher's administration of a standardized test and administration by a trained psychometrist.

The most compelling reason to avoid the use of standardized individual tests of achievement is that they do not provide the precise information which a teacher needs to plan an individualized program for a specific pupil. Survey tests of achievement are inappropriate because they sample too little of the possible content at each level—they have breadth but not depth—and do not allow one to pinpoint deficits and strengths. Two items of addition, for example, could be missed by chance rather than by reason of inadequate skills in addition. Even if the test is labeled as a *diagnostic* test (presumably having more items at each level of difficulty), the test may still be inappropriate for planning if it samples content other than that presented in the learner's classroom. Unless the measures selected for assessment of achievement sample the content actually presented daily in instruction, the teacher will gain information which is irrelevant to classroom purposes.

Examination of individual achievement tests which are specific to single content areas such as reading, spelling, or math will reveal that there are differences between these materials and the content presented in a given classroom. Test items constructed by subject matter specialists usually are based upon general curriculum content for each grade level, but they cannot reflect the specific content of the unique combination of texts and instructional practices employed in Mrs. Brown's fifth grade classroom. *The major limitation of published individual tests of achievement is not the construction of such tests or the skill of the teacher in administering them, but rather their variance from the tasks the student is asked to perform each day in a specific classroom.*

In addition to sampling content which is not directly applicable to a specific classroom, another disadvantage of formal tests is that standardized conditions do not allow for substitution of stimulus and response methods which might permit a student to use compensatory behaviors or special strengths which have been developed to cope with a disability. Every classroom teacher can testify that some students who seem to have a specific disability nevertheless manage to master academic work. They do so by working around their disability and finding ways to overcome it. A standardized test may require only oral presentation of arithmetic reasoning problems, which will penalize youngsters whose auditory memory is poor but who can handle the problem if they can see it. Learners who can spell orally but cannot form letters correctly because of motor impairment are penalized by a standardized test which requires written spelling to dictation.

Even if standardized tests could yield exactly the information which is needed, other reasons may preclude a teacher from being the best person to employ them. A teacher may have difficulty in conforming to standardized administration and in taking into account the test attitudes of the subject. Administration of standardized instruments requires a high degree of conformity. The test manual is to be followed rigidly with no deviations from prescribed procedure. Classroom teachers who are accustomed to modifying materials, altering instructions, and changing procedures in textbooks to suit their own classroom routine tend to consider publishers' directions as the point of departure for the teacher's own creative interpretation of the content. Creativity is not permitted in administration of standardized tests; yet the teacher's instincts may be at variance with the rigor demanded by the task.

Furthermore, classroom teachers do not have the clinician's experience to enable them to take into account the test attitudes of the subject. Although the student is likely to be receptive to testing by a known teacher instead of by an unknown psychometrist, the person with special training is in a better position to determine if any factors about the subject's behavior suggest that results may be invalid. The experience of the psychometrist will reveal the youngster who is so anxious, submissive, negativistic, stressful, or otherwise psychologically reacting to the testing as to impair problem-solving ability and thus invalidate the test results.

Certainly, there are advantages to formal, standardized instruments. Because procedures are predetermined, materials are collected, and tasks are arranged, the teacher need not make decisions or spend any time collecting or preparing items. He or she has only to pick up the instrument and use it. Also, the teacher can consult the manual for any questions about validity, reliability, standard error of measurement, or other questions relating to the qualification of the instrument, since the test constructors and the publisher have assumed this responsibility. In addition, results of standardized measures are readily communicated to other professional persons who are familiar with them, without the necessity of describing procedures or specifying task dimensions. Despite these advantages, which cannot be overlooked, the teacher who wishes to develop a useful program for an individual student is likely to find that informal measures using the classroom texts yield information which is more readily translated into lesson plans.

Informal Testing Using Classroom Materials

For purposes of describing an individual performance in basic skills areas, the testing of choice is that developed by the teacher from the classroom texts. If the teacher is actually using the classroom textbook items, rather than constructing items, this teacher is not likely to violate any principles of informal test construction. Since informal testing should examine behaviors which are as close as possible to the terminal behaviors the teacher wants the student to demonstrate in daily work, test items should be selected from the texts the student is to use in the classroom. When this approach is taken, questions of validity of test items need not be seriously considered.

The question of reliability over time, however, must be taken into account. The teacher must determine that a specific skills deficit is represented in the student's work as a reliable characteristic, to justify planning for remediation of that deficit. In informal as well as formal testing, the teacher must be able to recognize a random mistake as opposed to a consistent skill deficit. Fortunately, the teacher has the opportunity to base informal testing on analysis of work products, so this type of error is not likely in the teacher's informal testing.

The other consideration which the teacher must keep in mind is that, in general, a short test is less reliable than a test with more items. Suggestions for the number of items to be included are offered as each skills area is discussed in the following pages.

If informal testing is to yield useful information without usurping instructional time or becoming burdensome in preparation, it must be planned so that materials prepared for measuring skills levels can be used for all of the 10 to 12 students who may need to be tested in a given classroom. To be practical, informal measures must be designed so that a teacher has only to select those portions which apply to a given student; once the teacher develops a set of informal testing materials, they should make no further demands on teacher time for preparation. To be efficient, classroom testing also should follow at least five guidelines which must be kept in mind as informal evaluation is planned for a given student.

First, *only those skills which appear to be deficient need to be tested.* Information leading to this decision can be gained from three sources. The cumulative record of grades will yield relative strengths in subject matter areas. For example, a student may have shown strength by average or above-average grades in mathematics throughout the previous grades, while reading, spelling and writing have earned below-average grades. Arithmetic skills on group survey tests of achievement should then be checked to see if this pattern holds up, and both should be checked against the daily written products and response to group instruction which the teacher noted at the Identification stage. If these three sources of information indicate that only two or three skills areas need to be assessed in depth, the teacher's task is considerably lightened.

At a more refined level, the teacher's information at the Identification stage may have revealed that specific skills within subject matter areas are intact. For instance, a youngster may have indicated strengths in decoding skills in reading as measured by group tests, but relative weakness in comprehension. In such a case, the oral reading portion of the informal reading inventory may be omitted and only silent and listening capacity evaluated. In fact, if the student is above grade three and has demonstrated in the classroom that he or she can read silently with good comprehension, this student is exhibiting the skill needed in most language arts instruction in the intermediate grades or above, when oral reading will have been replaced by silent reading. To test skills which have been demonstrated as adequate, or those which will not be required in the classroom or in independent study, is inefficient.

Second, *testing is to proceed downward from the terminal behavior.* This means that the actual task which the student is expected to perform in the classroom, in its most complex form, should be presented first, rather than the subskills which are presumed to underlie the task. If the terminal behavior is to read orally a paragraph from the 3.2 basal reader, the teacher should not initially ask for a presentation of third grade words in isolation. Reading a list of words in isolation is not a classroom task, and this skill need not be tested if the student can demonstrate adequate reading of meaningful material in sentences. Only if the youngster cannot read the material in context should the teacher isolate specific words by presenting a word list. Similarly, if the student can read the words on a list in a flashed presentation, the teacher need not introduce them in an untimed presentation. Only those phonics skills which are indicated as possibly deficient by an analysis of oral reading errors should be checked against an informal phonics inventory.

For a mathematics sequence, testing should begin with the complex terminal behavior of solving a verbal problem stated in paragraph form, which involves reasoning to the correct operation, determining relevant information, placing numbers in proper slots within an operation, and computation. If this task cannot be performed, the next step down is to analyze the student's ability to solve sentence statements with missing elements. Computation of the basic operations in written form is a relatively simple task in this hierarchy, and it should be tested only if breakdowns are occurring at that level. If a student can successfully carry out mathematical reasoning and solution of problem sentences, the teacher may not need to test written computation of basic operations separately. Similarly, if a student can add and subtract with carrying, place value need not be checked; subtraction need not be tested separately if it is per-formed correctly in a series of division problems.

The teacher must make a distinction between the more com-plex task at a given level and a higher level task. For example, reading running text in a basal reader is a task more complex than reading a list of graded words, but each can be presented on the subject's independent or frustration reading level. Simi-larly, reasoning to the correct operation to be performed and computing the problem mentally is more complex than per-forming a computation in written form with the operation sign clearly present, but each can be performed with a variety of grade-level materials covering a range of difficulty.

The third guideline for efficiency is to *test most students in the classroom under typical classroom conditions during regular school hours.* Although scheduling must be carefully considered, as discussed below, a number of advantages favor one-to-one informal testing in the classroom with the other stu-dents present. First, testing in the classroom allows measurement of skills under the same conditions in which the student is expected to demonstrate those skills on a daily basis. Second, because testing in the classroom must take place in 10- or 20-minute segments of time, the teacher gains a more reliable esti-mate of skills at different times of the day and on different days. Although some testing must be conducted away from other pupils and under optimal conditions, it should be done only after the student has demonstrated that he or she cannot function appropriately under the regular classroom conditions.

The fourth guideline for efficiency is to *combine systematic observation of behavior with informal testing.* Not only the product of the task is of interest to the teacher, but also how the student arrived at the response. While the student is engaged in task behavior as part of an informal test of skills, the teacher must examine behavior closely. Such examination tells a teacher whether the youngster is primarily impulsive or deliberative, a planner or a trial-and-error learner, highly verbal or action-oriented, dependent upon aid or able to work alone, a risktaker who will attempt a solution at ceiling level or a cautious learner afraid to risk failure, reliant upon rote learning or able to reason to solutions, a master of skills at an automatic level or unsure of basic information and stumbling through tasks. All these characteristics and more have implications for planning the individualized program, and the teacher must be alert to the student's problem-solving style as well as absolute skill performance.

Close observation of behavior should not be limited to the one-to-one testing situation, however. Frequently, the youngster who appears to be task-oriented when working directly with the teacher will exhibit a number of interfering behaviors when working alone. For this reason, systematic observation of behavior should take place during independent seatwork and group instruction as well as in the one-to-one testing situation.

The teacher can proceed by pairing the target pupil with an average student in the class, and keeping a simple frequency count for a specified period of time of such behaviors as being out of seat, talking out, looking away from the book or the teacher, touching other students, or any other behavior which the teacher notes as inappropriate during the assigned task. By informally comparing a student at risk for failure with one who is achieving adequately, the teacher can get an estimate of the contribution of the interfering behaviors to the student's academic performance. This analysis also will assist the teacher in following through on the next guideline for efficiency.

The fifth guideline—to *separate skills deficits from environmental or behavioral conditions*—is related to both the third and fourth guidelines. The student who demonstrates a number of interfering behaviors under classroom conditions at seatwork or in one-to-one testing with the teacher must be given the opportunity to show what he or she can do under optimal conditions in a quiet room with no visual distractions. Only by re-presenting under ideal conditions those tasks which the student could not accomplish in the classroom can the teacher determine whether the learner exhibits a skills deficit or intact skills which cannot be demonstrated because of classroom conditions.

As the first step to establish which students and which skills require testing away from typical classroom conditions, work products should be evaluated in relation to behavior. If a student fails to complete written work, but is not noticeably off task or behaving inappropriately, the teacher has good reason to suspect that the products reflect the student's optimal performance and basic skills problems are suspect. If another student fails to complete work but also turns at sounds, watches everyone else work, daydreams, or engages in repetitive motor activity, it is not at all clear whether the uncompleted work is related to lack of skills, and this student should be tested one-to-one without other students present.

Similarly, if a student earns low grades on weekly spelling quizzes, but attends to the teacher's dictation, writes promptly and remains on task, he or she is less likely to require testing outside the classroom than the youngster who turns at every sound in the hall while the teacher is dictating, looks out the window instead of writing, then scrambles to see other pupils' papers. The student who is highly distractible or who exhibits a repertoire of interfering behaviors is the one whose skills must be tested under optimal, controlled conditions.

After the teacher has tentatively decided, from observation of behavior during seatwork and group instruction, that a specific student may need to be tested outside the classroom, he or she should check that perception against the student's performance in the one-to-one testing while the class is in session. Some students will be able to demonstrate their optimal performance if they are simply removed from the temptation of interacting with other pupils; being placed in one corner of the room with the teacher's undivided attention may be enough to allow them to work at their highest level. This decision must be made on a case-by-case basis. The important point to consider is that an instructional plan cannot be drawn up until the teacher is satisfied that he or she knows the status of basic skills deficits with the variable of distraction removed as much as is possible.

SCHEDULE FOR CLASSROOM TESTING

Precise scheduling is required if 10 to 12 students within a classroom are to be given informal testing early enough in the year to make use of the information for most of the instructional term. But scheduling is not enough—the teacher will need some assistance from peer or parent volunteers, paid aides, or administrators. As soon as the teacher has drawn up a list of the students who require academic testing and a tentative daily schedule for testing, he or she should estimate the need for regular help in the classroom. If approximately 90 minutes of testing per day are scheduled, for example, the teacher will want to ask for two hours of aide time so students who are not to be tested will receive their share of instructional attention.

The advantage of scheduling the individual diagnostic testing to follow immediately upon the Identification stage is that much of the work which is covered in the first six weeks of instruction is likely to be review material rather than unfamiliar concepts or new skills. In attempting to complete the Identification stage within the first month and the individual diagnosis within the second month of the term, the teacher should be able to delegate some review sessions to paraprofessionals or volunteers.

Some schools provide a pool of aide or volunteer time and teachers may bid for it. Of course, the time most in demand is the heavy academic period early in the morning when most reading groups are in session. By selecting the less attractive late morning or early afternoon times, a teacher may be able to obtain more help. If a school has no pool of assistants, a teacher might enlist the aid of the principal in requesting parent volunteers or older students who could be released from class during library time or independent work time.

Testing During Class Time

Testing can be conducted during class time in two ways. First, the teacher can allocate time already set aside for small groups, such as oral reading time. While the classroom aide works with the small group and the remainder of the class is occupied with independent work, the teacher can take one student from the reading group to administer the informal reading inventory, substituting the test for the pupil's reading lesson that day. The same plan can be followed if students are in small groups for math instruction. Time already set aside for small-group instruction is not time taken from class supervision, so most teachers can easily fit testing into periods when a small group can be managed by an assistant.

The second possibility is testing while the entire class is engaged in independent seatwork. After the teacher has presented a group lesson and the students are engaged in an application activity, the aide could supervise by circulating among the students while the teacher takes one pupil aside. If the seatwork period is lengthy, the teacher might be able to test two youngsters during this time, and circulate among the students between testing sessions.

Since the certified teacher is in the room at all times, the paraprofessional or volunteer is able to assist, but the teacher does not abdicate responsibility for what is happening in the classroom. Testing conducted in the classroom should be done in a location where the teacher is facing the class but the student is facing the teacher and a blank wall. The teacher should be able to see the activity in the room, but should not respond to events except in case of emergency. The student who is being tested should have the teacher's attention; the other pupils are instructed to seek help from the aide. Testing may be done at the teacher's desk, at a small desk in a corner of the room, or at any table or desk which is not in use. A screen need not be erected for the pupil's testing unless the teacher believes it is warranted.

In order to complete testing over reading, mathematics, spelling and writing during class time, the teacher must be willing to obtain information in 10- to 20- minute segments. Because most students attend better if work is presented in small units, this time frame will be no disadvantage to the student, and the teacher will likewise find advantages in seeing a given youngster perform in a one-to-one situation over a series of days. If Susan is presented a 20- minute segment of the informal reading inventory on Monday morning during reading group, and another 10 minutes on Tuesday, the teacher has a chance to check the reliability of errors in decoding skills. If the mathematics inventory is presented on Monday morning and Tuesday afternoon, the teacher can see whether fatigue late in the day results in a different performance over similar tasks.

Breaking testing into small units requires close attention to detail, however, so that one portion of a test is not inadvertently omitted. A set of worksheets should be designed by the teacher, to allow marking of testing completed and to have an immediate reference to determine what is to be presented next to a given student.

Testing During Released Time

The teacher will find it necessary to structure some released time when he or she is not responsible for other students, to re-present tasks under optimal conditions to a few students whose skills cannot be adequately assessed under classroom conditions. This can be done by making use of time when students are out of the room, or by taking the student to another room while someone else supervises the class.

The most obvious time to be set aside for testing is the teacher's planning period, when the class is out of the room. Many teachers may be able to devote planning time to testing over a three- or four-week period without risking inadequate preparation for instruction. Since instruction preparation can be done after school hours, teachers should be able to allocate at least part of the weekly planning time to individual testing during the Diagnosis stage, because students are available during this period. The teacher simply retains in the classroom the youngster who is to be tested, and administers the one-to-one testing without distractions. If the class is scheduled for physical education, art, or music in other than the regular classroom, or if the students have designated times to go to the library with a librarian in attendance, these periods may present blocks of time to be used for individual testing.

Another way to secure released time for testing is to enlist the help of personnel who are certified but who do not have the responsibility of a class. For example, the counselor or the vice principal may be able to supervise a class for 30 minutes during independent seatwork to allow the teacher to take a single learner out for testing. The provision of released time by other professionals assuming a teacher's supervisory role might increase if the teacher could persuade them that such a plan would result in more precise referral questions and improved individualized programs. It is probably a mistake to suggest that teacher diagnosis will result in a decrease in referrals, although it may in fact do so. Instead, *the administration must be persuaded of the intrinsic value of a teacher's diagnosis of academic status,* and that more precise testing, rather than less testing, will be the result.

INFORMAL CLASSROOM INVENTORIES

Informal Reading Inventory

The informal reading inventory based upon materials actually in use in the classroom is the best method of establishing which textbook can be placed in Tim's hands on Monday morning. Although a limited number of informal tests which are available can prove useful for diagnostic purposes, classroom texts remain the ultimate measure of what the student can do in Mrs. Brown's fifth grade. The most compelling reason to use the classroom texts to measure reading skills is the lack of correspondence between those results and results of any other test using material drawn from standard word lists or readability formulas. A published test may have been devised according to a readability formula different from the one used for the adopted reading series; the published word list may be drawn from sources other than the contextual material; sentence structure may be controlled in different ways.

A published informal reading inventory which accompanies the adopted basal text can be the basis for the teacher's informal inventory, if he or she prefers to save the time involved in developing one. But the published inventories are seldom as comprehensive as they could be. They do not typically include three passages for oral, silent and listening capacity at each level; they often do not select word lists from the paragraphs to be read; and instructions seldom include flashed as well as untimed presentation of word lists. If the guidelines which are offered here for preparation of an informal inventory are used to modify the published inventory, such changes will allow the publisher's version to yield more information and yet save time for the teacher.

To be absolutely precise about the construction and administration of an informal reading inventory, the publisher's reported grade levels for the adopted series should be checked against a standard readability formula. But this is essential only if the teacher expects to translate the student's instructional reading level to material other than the basal reader. Because publishers make use of different readability formulas to determine the reading level of texts, one cannot transfer the reading level of a reader by one publisher to a social studies text by another publisher. But establishing readability takes too much time to expect the teacher to do so for purposes of the informal reading inventory alone. Instead, the teachers might join together and work with the reading specialist to derive readability levels for each of the textbook series adopted in the building, as part of their instructional program. Or this information may already be available from the textbook selection committee which recommended the series.

To develop the informal reading inventory, the following steps might be pursued.

1. Select three passages from the beginning of at least seven levels of the basal reading series. For example, a third-grade teacher should select from the first reader, the 2.1, 2.2, 3.1, 3.2, 4.1, and 4.2 readers in order to have an

adequate range around the nominal grade level. The selections should be made from the beginning of the book because the entry level to that book is to be appraised. Three passages should be chosen from each book—one for oral reading, one for silent reading, and one for listening capacity.

The length of the passages varies with the grade level. At preprimer and primer levels, 50 words in each passage will be an adequate selection; from grades 1 through 4, 100 words are enough; above grade 4, 150 to 200 words should be selected; for junior high, 250 words should be used. Words should be counted accurately for computation of word recognition scores, but they will not necessarily be the suggested round figures, since a given passage should always close at the end of the sentence nearest the round figure word count. Thus, computation of instructional level may be based on 95% of 248 or 253 words.

2. Arrange for a recording copy of each passage. This can be as simple as a second copy of the text with a piece of acetate on which errors can be recorded. But it is preferable to have a typed copy which allows room for notation of errors. The typed copy may be laminated to allow the teacher to write on it and reuse it, or a spirit master could be made to maintain a supply of duplicated pages. The recording copy should be triple spaced to permit notation of error. A notation system to mark omissions, substitutions, insertions, repetitions, and examiner pronunciations can be obtained from a standard reading text. The teacher's record sheet also should allow space for verbatim responses to comprehension questions according to a number designation.

3. Prepare comprehension questions for each passage at each level. At least four comprehension questions should

follow each passage, and more should be provided for subjects above fourth grade. One question should request a *definition of a word* in the context of the passage: "What does the word *harbor* mean in this sentence?" One question should require *immediate recall* of a fact stated in the passage: "What time of day did Jim leave his house? Another question should require the student to *draw an inference* from facts stated in the selection: "Was Jim happy or sad about moving to a new house?" A fourth question should require a *statement of the main idea or a conclusion* to be drawn from the passage: "What would be a good title for this story?" or "What did Jim learn about making friends?"

In addition, *sequencing* ability should be measured by asking the subject to retell one or two passages in the order in which the events occurred. *Ability to predict outcomes* should be measured by pausing between passages to ask: "What do you think will happen next?" This is most effective when the passage selected in the book for oral reading is followed directly in the book by the passage selected for silent reading. Verbatim responses to questions should be recorded.

4. Begin the presentation of the first oral passage at a level which is the teacher's best estimate of the student's reading level, on the basis of classroom work. If this passage is too difficult, drop down immediately to an easier level and work up. Time the student's oral reading with a stopwatch, record the time to the nearest second, and follow immediately with oral presentation of comprehension questions.

5. Follow the oral reading at each level with the silent passage, which is also timed with a stopwatch. Proceed with alternate oral and silent passages, each followed by comprehension questions, until the student's word recog-

nition falls below 95% and comprehension falls below 75%.

6. When the highest instructional reading level has been reached on oral reading, present the third passage at that level by reading it to the student and asking the comprehension questions. Proceed with reading of the listening capacity passages until the student's comprehension of passages read falls below 75%.

7. Select 20% of the words from the three passages at each level to comprise a list of words in isolation to follow the paragraph reading. The best method of selection is to divide the number of words needed, say 20 at 3rd grade, into the number of words in the three passages at that level, 300. This formula results in the figure 15. Then, every 15th word from the three passages of book 3.2, for example, should be selected for the word list. If duplications occur, use the next word on the line.

Although the traditional administration presents the word list *before* the oral paragraph is read in order to determine the entry level for oral paragraph reading, the general plan of testing down from the more complex behavior would dictate that the list of words in isolation be presented only when the paragraph reading falls below instructional level or 95% word recognition. The reasoning is that if the student can read correctly in context, which is the behavior to be carried out in the classroom, there is no need to examine ability to read lists of words in isolation, which is not a classroom task. However, at the point where word recognition falls below instructional level, the purpose of reading words in isolation *after* paragraph reading is to obtain additional diagnostic information from the types of substitutions which are made. Two word lists should be presented: the one at the highest instructional level reached by the student on the inventory, and one level above that.

Present word lists first at a flashed rate of one-half second exposure, and follow with a second untimed presentation of any words which were not recognized when flashed. This procedure provides a measure of the words known at the automatic level and those which can be decoded when word attack methods are applied.

8. Analyze word recognition errors from paragraph reading and from reading of word lists. Determine the percentage of substitutions, omissions, insertions, mispronunciations, repetitions, and teacher-aided pronunciations. Establish patterns of graphic/phonic errors which should be investigated further by means of a published or teacher-developed phonics inventory. Determine the percentage of literal, inferential, main idea, and vocabulary comprehension questions missed. Compute the word recognition scores and comprehension scores for each level of paragraph reading to verify the instructional and listening capacity levels, and the independent level, if established. Compute the reading rate in terms of words per minute. Record this information for purposes of a status report and as pretest data for programming.

Analysis of Reading Performance

At a minimum, the reading inventory should establish two reading levels: Instructional—the level for classroom materials to be read under the teacher's direction, established at 95% word recognition and 75% comprehension; Listening Capacity—the highest level of readability at which the learner understands the vocabulary and sentence structure of material read aloud by the teacher, established at 75% comprehension. A third level—Independent—the level at which a pupil can read supplementary materials or library books without aid at 98% word recognition and 90% comprehension. This should be determined for older students but it may not yet be established among primary students.

To proceed with the analysis, the following questions should be addressed.

— What is the student's potential instructional reading level? That is, how well can this pupil be expected to read with adequate remedial instruction? This question is answered by comparing the listening capacity level against the present instructional level. The listening capacity level is considered a good estimate of the potential instructional level because the pupil can understand the vocabulary and sentence structure even though he or she cannot comprehend it visually due to word recognition problems. If a student comprehended materials read to him or her with 75% comprehension at the 6.2 level but is now instructional at 4.2, the 6.2 reader is a realistic goal for remedial instruction the teacher will plan for a pupil with adequate vision.

— What is the pattern of reading errors? Is the student characterized as a context reader who lacks decoding skills but grasps the main idea of the passage and reads at a good rate? Or is the learner a word-caller whose word-recognition skills are strong but who disregards phrasing and punctuation, reads slowly, and misses the point of the passages?

Computing a simple frequency percentage of the different types of oral reading errors can reveal the student's reading "personality." The pupil who demonstrates 50% substitutions (all real words), 25% mispronunciations, and 25% insertions is willing to experiment; this student guesses on the basis of meaning, and comprehension is likely to be quite good though word attack skills are lacking. The pupil who exhibits 50% omissions, 25% teacher pronunciations, and 25% substitutions is a cautious reader who will not attempt a word if it cannot be recognized at sight; and this student has not learned to predict a probable word on the basis of the meaning or sentence structure of the passage. However, such precision will present an advantage over the first reader in learning word attack skills. Analysis of percentages of types of errors, combined with comprehension scores and reading rates, will yield an overall picture of the type of reader who is to be instructed.

— What types of cues does the reader use most frequently or fail to take into account in the reading performance? This is answered by a detailed examination of the types of *oral* errors, which tend to fall into three categories:

- Overreliance on or failure to use content or meaning cues: The student omits, inserts, or substitutes a word or phrase, distorting the *sense* of the passage.
- Disregard for syntactic or word-order cues: The pupil omits, inserts, or substitutes a word or alters word order, distorting the *grammar* of the passage.
- Inattention to graphic/phonic cues: The student inserts a word which has no graphic counterpart, omits a printed word, or substitutes a word which is *graphically* unrelated to the printed word.

If a reader is making use of context to the exclusion of other cues, the substitution will sometimes be of the type: (Substitutions are shown in italics.)

bucket
He filled the   pail   with water.

If such errors are infrequent, they can be overlooked, because the reader has grasped the meaning of the passage. But such errors are serious if they occur in science or math materials where precision is essential.

Failure to make adequate use of context cues frequently results in substitutions which are nonsense words, such as,

prif
He filled the pail with water.

Such substitutions indicate a failure to check the decoded word against the student's own oral vocabulary as well as against the meaning of the passage. Disregard of context may also involve real words, as in,

part   *watches*
He filled the pail with   water   .

Errors of this type are typically accompanied by comprehension problems and this reader is characterized as a "word-caller." The student is likely to demonstrate an inadequate oral vocabulary, since he or she sometimes accepts words which are not real English words.

Disregard of syntax or word order results in substitutions outside the appropriate word class, such as a noun for a verb, or omission of function words such as articles or prepositions. A production such as

pull what went
He filled the pail with water.

is an exaggerated version of this type of error. The reader does not check reading performance against grammatical competence and uses the verbs *pull* and *went* in noun slots and the pronoun *what* in a preposition slot. A reader who could use syntactic cues would predict on the basis of form class what the word is likely to be and narrow the range of possible substitutions to the same form class as the printed word. An error pattern which disregards syntax may indicate a general language disorder.

Inattention to graphic/phonic cues can result in an error of the type,

pan
He filled the pail with water.

in which the sense and the syntax are intact but only the initial portion of the graphic symbol has been used to decode the word. Probably the highest proportion of word recognition errors falls into the category of substitutions based on inadequate graphic/phonic information. Most such errors are mispronunciations, but omissions can also result from inattention to graphic cues.

The classification of oral reading errors into these three groups does not suggest that they are mutually exclusive. Indeed, most readers are characterized by two or more types of errors. But the frequency pattern allows the teacher to describe more precisely the characteristics of an individual reader. In addition to this breakdown of errors, specific phonics and visual decoding skills must be analyzed from the oral reading passages, or determined on the basis of the scope and sequence chart for the adopted series or by a published or teacher-developed informal phonics survey.

— What is the relationship among types of comprehension questions answered and missed? If a student correctly answered 100% of the factual questions but missed all the inference questions and 50% of the vocabulary questions, he or she will need a type of instruction quite different from the pupil who answered only 50% of the factual questions but 100% of the vocabulary and inference questions. The first student is a literal reader who may lack a background of experience and who cannot make good use of recall to build problem-solving techniques. The second student is not sufficiently attentive to detail but can develop the meaning of words from context and build on the facts recalled in order to reason to additional information. This type of analysis must be used to develop study guides or other aids to comprehension for specific students, since the pattern of comprehension errors carries a great many implications for a plan of instruction.

— What is the relationship between oral reading rate and silent reading rate? In a mature reader, the silent reading rate should always be faster than the oral rate. The same relationship exists for the context reader. If silent rate is not faster, the pupil may be overanalyzing words by dependence upon graphic/phonic cues to the exclusion of other cues. Or the reader may lack an adequate sight vocabulary of frequently used words. The silent reading rate should be examined against the relative fluency of oral reading. If hesitations, repetitions, or disregard of punctuation characterized oral reading, the same habits may be barriers to silent reading. Vocalization during silent reading is also responsible for slower rate.

— Upon examination of the lists of single words in isolation which followed paragraph reading, what is the relationship between the flashed word recognition score and the untimed word recognition score? If the two scores are similar, the student lacks word analysis techniques since he or she cannot improve the score by taking time to decode an unknown word. If the two scores differ and the reader recognized more words when given additional time, the student has demonstrated the ability to use word attack skills.

At the instructional level, the relationship betwen the word recognition score for paragraph reading and the score for words in isolation is a measure of the reader's ability to use context cues. The score should be higher for material read in context, since the reader has access to meaning and grammatical cues as well as the graphic/phonic cues presented by the isolated word list.

— What is the percentage of self-corrected errors? A student who allows errors of word recognition which violate the sense and the grammatical integrity of sentences to stand without correction is quite different from the reader who corrects his or her own errors along the way. The first reader does not provide self-monitoring of performance, is likely to be less involved in the reading process, and probably is not motivated to read either for information or for enjoyment. The second reader is actively engaged in the reading process, is more likely to be reading with purpose, and certainly is making use of context and grammatical cues to decode unfamiliar words. The self-corrected error usually is not counted for purposes of establishing error rates for reading levels, on the theory that the self-correction is a strength which indicates strategies for drawing meaning from graphic symbols.

— Are oral reading substitutions in syntactic or graphic/phonic areas consistent with patterns of a dialect of English, perhaps one of the black English dialects? Such patterns might include omission of inflections, as on possessives, plurals or verb tenses; omission of auxiliary verbs; insertion of a redundant pronoun as in "The boy he went"; or insertion of double negatives. Vowel substitutions also may reflect dialect pronunciations. When the reader is a dialect speaker, the teacher must be able to distinguish word-recognition errors from spontaneous translation into dialect English.

Any number of additional relationships can be explored to yield a profile of an individual reader. For purposes of describing the student's skills preparatory to planning the individualized program, the above analysis would provide a great deal of useful information, but the reading analysis can be extended to the limit of the individual teacher's understanding of the reading process.

Informal Mathematics Inventory

Although it does not parallel the informal reading inventory, an informal mathematics inventory can be constructed, using several levels of the adopted mathematics text. Since no readability formulas or similar guides to the selection of graded materials for testing in arithmetic are available, the content which the publisher has placed in the adopted texts cannot readily be checked to determine if placement of concepts and operations is at appropriate grade levels.

If scope and sequence charts are available for several widely used texts, these charts can be combined with survey tests of arithmetic achievement to see whether the adopted text is a relatively difficult or easy text. Diagnostic information, combined with the teacher's knowledge that the adopted text appears to present many concepts and operations earlier than other texts, or presents multiple concepts simultaneously, should affect the rate at which the teacher decides to present the material when the program is written, as well as the amount of practice she requires before moving on. Of course, a textbook review committee may already have information to show the relationship of the adopted text to other available materials. Regardless of how this information is gained, *the teacher must have a perspective on the difficulty level of the content of the adopted text before using it to judge performance in mathematics.*

Although many teachers may feel comfortable testing computation skills in basic operations as a measure of status in mathematics, such testing should be used for *additional* diagnostic information after evaluation of higher-level skills has been conducted. The type of mathematics inventory suggested here is not, of course, the only format which could be followed to gain informal information about skills. The sequence of testing in mathematics is interpreted differently on the basis of one's theoretical approach to the organization of content in mathematics. One possible set of steps in an informal mathematics inventory is proposed as follows.

1. Test downward from the complex to the simple by starting with word problems. According to one type of organization of content, the most complex task would be the solution of verbal problems stated in paragraph form, requiring several steps. The learner must identify the question to be answered, determine the given facts which are needed to answer it, and select the operation which would express the relationship between what is known and what is to be found. He or she must then visualize or write the relationship in the form of an open mathematical sentence and finally solve it by computation.

2. Select word problems from several grade levels of the adopted mathematics text. For example, a fifth grade teacher should have texts for grades 2, 3, and 4, in addition to 5. Select from the middle one-third of each level. Sampling the content of an arithmetic series differs from sampling reading in that the organization of the math text is such that a logical sequence and a hierarchy of operations proceeds through the text. Avoid review material at the beginning of the book, and sample only the grade-level content typically introduced about one-third into the text. This method should establish entry to a specific level of the adopted series.

3. Draw two verbal paragraph problems from each of the middle three or four chapters of each level of the text. Be sure to sample a range of the material presented in those chapters in terms of different operations required

and number of operations required in a single problem. This method will result in selection of 6 or 8 problems from each level of the adopted text, for a total of approximately 24 problems over 3 or 4 levels.

4. Analyze each selected word problem and write open mathematical sentences to describe the operation(s) involved in each. Expressing the result to be found as the open element in each mathematical sentence, write more than one sentence if alternative methods of solution are possible.

5. Rewrite each mathematical sentence in step 4 as a problem for computation, complete with the sign for the appropriate operation.

6. Write or type each word problem, open mathematical sentence, and computation problem on a separate 3″ x 5″ or 5″ x 7″ index card. This procedure allows flexibility in using the materials, since they can be combined in many ways; it also allows the student to deal with only one problem at a time, with attendant motivation instead of the frustration which sometimes accompanies presentation of too much work at one time. Devise a numbering or marking system to correlate the mathematical sentences and computation problems with the word problems, so that three sets of related cards are the result.

7. Cover each card with clear plastic or have it laminated so answers can be written with a wax pencil directly on the card and retained for analysis, then removed so the card can be reused by another pupil. This procedure carries two benefits. First, it forces the teacher to analyze materials promptly following testing, since there is no permanent mimeographed copy to be placed in the file and forgotten. Second, it saves considerable clerical time and the paper required to duplicate numerous items for 10 or more pupils who might have to be evaluated.

8. Begin with the grade-level text which is the teacher's best estimate of the learner's level from analysis of work products at the Identification stage. If the student is not

successful on the first four word problems, drop down to the next lower level.

9. Ask the student to read the verbal paragraph problems aloud if able to do so. This is essential so the teacher can check the accuracy of the information the learner is processing. The teacher should follow the reading on the textbook copy. If the student reads with less than 95% word recognition, the teacher should read each problem aloud and allow the student to follow along on the card copy to avoid being penalized by lack of graphic figures available to students who can read the problems themselves.

10. After each problem has been read, ask the student to solve it in any way he or she sees fit. Provide extra paper if needed, and retain any computations for later analysis. If the learner can successfully solve the verbal problem, set the card aside to indicate that it has been mastered. For any problems which have not been solved successfully directly from the word problem, move to the next step.

11. For every verbal problem-solving task which was not solved correctly, isolate the components by asking the student to go through his or her thinking processes. Ask questions to discover the student's strategies: "What is the question? What numbers do we have to answer it? What do we do with the numbers? What number is missing? Call the missing number n; can you write a sentence to show where n belongs? This type of inquiry should isolate the point of breakdown in the reasoning process. Care should be taken to ensure that the inquiry does not result in supplying information. The inquiry is designed to test, not to teach.

12. If the verbal inquiry does not lead the student to solve the problem, the related cards for the next lower level of complexity, solving open mathematical sentences, should be presented. The student should be asked to solve the sentence without aid and to write the answer on the

card. If he or she requests aid, use an inquiry method as above to determine the information being used without giving additional cues.

13. For each problem which cannot be solved at the level of the open mathematical sentence, present the card showing the problem in computation form. Ask the student to compute and write the answer on the card.

At this point in the inventory, the teacher should have an impression of the student's relative abilities with verbal problems, open mathematical sentences, and computation at a single level of the adopted text. Depending upon the teacher's criterion for mastery, he or she can now estimate the student's instructional level in mathematics. For example, if the overall performance across word problems, open sentences, and computation was 80% or above at grade 4, the teacher may consider him or her instructional at grade 5. An overall performance lower than 80% at the middle of the fourth grade book probably indicates that the student should work through that book, or at that level of difficulty in supplementary materials.

For additional diagnostic information, the teacher can probe the hierarchy of skills in each operation below those presented at the instructional level. For example, if the student's performance on the inventory indicates that he or she is instructional in the third grade math text, skills which are presented in the series below grade three might be explored to isolate the weak components in operations the student could not perform. This can be done by sampling categories of skills within addition, subtraction, multiplication, or division from the complex to the simple, selecting computation problems from the lower levels of the text.

For addition, the sequence might be something like this:

Carrying in alternate columns with zeros: 56060
                                          27358
                                          ‾‾‾‾‾

Carrying from tens *and* ones places: 139
                                       182
                                       ‾‾‾

Carrying from tens *or* ones place:　380　156
　　　　　　　　　　　　　　　　　　　70　234
　　　　　　　　　　　　　　　　　　　——　——

No carrying:　13
　　　　　　　26
　　　　　　　——

For subtraction, the sequence might be: Regrouping in alternate columns with zeros; regrouping in hundreds and tens places; regrouping in tens or ones place; no regrouping.

For multiplication, the hierarchy could cover: Three or more digits, including zeros, with carrying; two digits, with zeros and carrying; carrying from three places, carrying from two places; carrying from ones to tens place; no carrying.

For division, a possible sequence is: Three or more digits with zeros and remainders; two digits with zeros and remainders; uneven division with zeros and remainders; uneven division without remainders; even division.

Move from the symbolic to the pictorial to the concrete if response warrants. If a pupil can manipulate symbolic (*3* or *three*) material, the teacher need not move downward to the pictorial or the concrete manipulative levels. Only if the student demonstrates that he or she cannot deal with the higher levels using numerals in operations should it be necessary to check the understanding of "threeness" which can be done by matching pictorial or manipulative objects in sets.

A similar sequence could be followed for operations on fractions and decimals. When such a set of computation items is selected from the text for diagnostic testing, enough samples of each operation should be selected to establish mastery or to provide data for identification of error patterns or faulty algorithms. No specific number of items has been generally agreed upon to provide reliable testing. However, two problems in each subcategory of division listed above would total 10 problems, which should be sufficient to sample an operation. The teacher's judgment can be a guide to a number which will not exhaust the student and which the teacher can reasonably analyze. To conserve the teacher's one-to-one testing time, the probe portion of the mathematics sample can be presented as independent seatwork at a time when the teacher is circulating and thus can observe task behavior of the testee and also supervise other students.

Analysis of Mathematics Performance

Error patterns in mathematics performance can occur in at least three major ways, singly or in combination:

1. Inadequate facts: Using a correct operation and a sound strategy, the pupil applies inaccurate addition, subtraction, or multiplication facts.
2. Incorrect operation: Using accurate facts, the learner subtracts rather than adding or divides instead of multiplying.
3. Ineffective strategy: Using the proper operation and accurate facts, the learner applies steps out of sequence, skips steps, or applies a tactic which does not always result in a correct outcome.

Inadequate recall of facts is probably the most frequent type of error because many students have never mastered the primary facts. Recall of basic facts must operate at the automatic level—a student must recall the fact without "figuring it out" by any means—if arithmetic computation is to be efficient and reliable. Some straightforward facts errors are:

$$
\begin{array}{cccc}
4 & 9 & 34 & 88 \\
\underline{+5} & \underline{-3} & \underline{\times 2} & 3\overline{)275} \\
8 & 5 & 98 & \underline{25} \\
& & & 25 \\
& & & \underline{25}
\end{array}
$$

Reasoning to an incorrect operation in a word problem usually is associated with failure to grasp whether a part or a whole is to be found; it represents an inadequate conceptualization of the problem. At the computation level, an incorrect operation can result from a misreading of the symbols for operations, as in

$$\begin{array}{r} 21 \\ \times 13 \\ \hline 34 \end{array}.$$

More frequently, it results from temporary inattention to the task in the midst of the problem. For example, a pupil computing

$$\begin{array}{r} 261 \\ \times 35 \\ \hline 1305 \\ 783 \\ \hline 9105 \end{array} \text{ and } \begin{array}{r} 430 \\ \times 15 \\ \hline 2150 \\ 430 \\ \hline 6450 \end{array}$$

clearly lost track of the task on the first computation, since the student later demonstrated correct addition using zeros. But if such patterns recur as in

$$\begin{array}{r} 26 \\ -10 \\ \hline 10 \end{array} \text{ or } \begin{array}{r} 20 \\ +28 \\ \hline 40 \end{array}$$

they are often associated with confusion about the role of zero or one in addition, subtraction, and multiplication.

Application of an ineffective strategy can be as basic as serial counting in place of addition as in

$$\begin{array}{r} 4 \\ 5 \\ \hline 6 \end{array}$$

or as complex as adding a regrouped number to a column without completing the multiplication:

$$\begin{array}{r} 24 \\ \times 6 \\ \hline 44 \end{array}.$$

Errors in the first two categories (inadequate facts and incorrect operation) may be more frequent and cause as many problems, but errors in the third category are more serious because they arise from misunderstanding of or misapplication of algorithms. A pupil may respond to intensive developmental teaching to learn basic facts, and can be taught by developmental measures to recognize the appropriate operation; but if a learner is using an ineffective strategy, the inefficient method must be extinguished before it can be replaced with a sound strategy. For this reason, the ineffective processes followed by the student in arriving at the answer must be analyzed in detail if appropriate remedial programs are to be designed.

The following questions might be asked:

— What is the relationship between the performance in written computation and solution of word problems? If a student lacks reading skills or oral language skills to manipulate verbal symbols but can compute successfully if the problem is reduced to manipulation of numbers, implications for remediation are not the same as for a student who can read and reason to the correct operation for word problems but lacks basic facts for computation, or for the learner who cannot solve the problem in either form. The first student has technical skills in arithmetic which must be matched by verbal skills; the second can think quantitatively but requires practice in basic operations; the third may be demonstrating a global disorder in mathematics or may simply be working at a level above his or her capability.

— What is the contribution of observed reading problems to the lack of mastery? If attempts at oral reading of word problems revealed substitutions which would alter the interpretation of the problem, the student may be processing inaccurate information which could account for erroneous results. For example, if key words such as *sold, found, divided, times, each,* or *total* are misread, the student cannot engage in sound verbal reasoning.

— Did the verbal inquiry reveal that the learner lacks the vocabulary of mathematical terms to express the problem in conventional terminology? Sometimes a student who is asked to describe how he or she worked a problem will elect instead to demonstrate the solution with numbers. If the one-to-one interaction with the student suggested a lack of vocabulary for mathematics notation, the student needs opportunities to clarify and use the language of mathematics so problem solving can be aided by mediational language. Remain alert to the contribution of terminology if the learner cannot *describe* the process he or she followed.

— Does evidence suggest that the learner is not able to conceptualize quantitative experience? If, for example, the student could not determine whether a part or a whole was to be found, could compute

$$6 + 4 = \square \quad \text{but not} \quad (3+2+1) + (2+1+1) = \square$$

or made basic errors in seriation, one-to-one correspondence, or discrimination of greater or lesser quantities, he or she may be exhibiting an inability to think in quantitative terms. With this type of evidence, evaluation with pictorial or concrete materials is indicated.

— Is the result of the student's computation a reasonable estimate of the correct answer? In other words, is the learner capable of approximating the figure which would result from a correct computation? There is a considerable difference between a learner whose incorrect answer is 10 times or ½ the correct figure, and the student whose incorrect response is a rounded estimate of the correct result. The first student may not be able to conceptualize the problem in terms of whether a portion is to be added or taken away. If incorrect answers reflect distance from the range or the number of digits in the correct response, the learner lacks the ability to estimate.

— Do incorrect responses fit patterns of unusual computational algorithms? Can specific ineffective strategies which are responsible for repeated failure be identified? If so, extinguishing that algorithm and replacing it with a workable alternative can be a straightforward solution for some learners. For example, the student who computed:

$$
\begin{array}{cc}
\begin{array}{r}
44 \\
5\overline{)216} \\
20 \\
\hline
16 \\
16 \\
\hline
\end{array}
&
\begin{array}{r}
85 \\
6\overline{)526} \\
48 \\
\hline
46 \\
40 \\
\hline
6
\end{array}
\end{array}
$$

has used a faulty strategy: dividing the first number in the quotient into the second number in the dividend. Using the wrong divisor is a pattern which can be identified and changed.

— Do errors fit a pattern of spatial disorientation or directional confusion? Apparent errors of fact sometimes can be traced to simple directional reversals. For example,

$$\begin{array}{r} 12 \\ \times 4 \\ \hline 84 \end{array} \qquad \begin{array}{r} 34 \\ \times 2 \\ \hline 86 \end{array}$$

fit a pattern of transposition of products rather than errors of fact. A common error in subtraction with borrowing

$$\begin{array}{r} 24 \\ -18 \\ \hline 4 \end{array}$$

may represent a misunderstanding about the direction of the operation.

— What proportion of computation errors are random or careless mistakes as opposed to systematic errors? For example, careless mistakes of these types might occur.

Omitting a numeral in addition:

$$\begin{array}{r} 3 \\ 6 \\ 5 \\ \hline 11 \end{array} \qquad \begin{array}{r} 8 \\ 5 \\ 2 \\ \hline 13 \end{array}$$

Writing an incomplete answer:

$$\begin{array}{r} 72 \\ 51 \\ \hline 23 \end{array} \qquad \begin{array}{r} 329 \\ -15 \\ \hline 14 \end{array}$$

Omitting part of the operation:

$$\begin{array}{r} 53 \\ +35 \\ \hline 58 \end{array} \qquad \begin{array}{r} 87 \\ -23 \\ \hline 84 \end{array}$$

These errors indicate no faulty facts, improper strategies or incorrect operations. They seem to result instead from inattention to the task or distraction from the task at hand. Observation of task behavior might permit identification of the environmental factors which contribute to such random errors; and motivational strategies, rather than remedial instruction, may be the treatment of choice.

Informal Writing Sample

Writing is a language task, but it is a secondary language skill, dependent upon the primary skill—oral language. Before writing is sampled, it may be helpful to separate the *verbal* formulation task, or oral language competence, from the *written* formulation task, since different combinations of skills are involved. The language evaluation might begin, therefore, with a brief sample of the learner's oral language. The teacher can elicit such a sample by asking any one or a series of open-ended questions which cannot be answered with a fragment or a *yes* or *no* response. "Tell me about your best friend," or "I'd like to hear about your pets" constrain sentences in response. If oral and written samples are to be compared, it is useful to ask the same question for both: "Tell me about what happened at school yesterday."

The oral language sample should be recorded on tape for later analysis. A two-minute sample from the middle of a five-minute tape is adequate to gain an overall impression of oral language status. The teacher should listen for examples of structures which might be associated with a chronologically younger learner, such as, "Her writed on the board;" omission of auxiliary verbs or tense markers as in, "He walk to the gym;" confusion of word order, as in, "Music we go first." The teacher also should note marked hesitations or unusual word substitutions which might indicate that vocabulary is deficient or not readily retrieved. The teacher should attend to any structures or pronunciations which might signal a dialect speaker. In addition, the teacher should be alert to any usage which might suggest verbalisms (use of words without understanding of the meaning attached). By listening to the two-minute sample again at a later time, the teacher can compare the language to standard English usage.

In evaluating writing skills, one must separate the *language formulation* task from the *motor execution* task. Since a written message can be analyzed from the point of view of both content and form, the teacher requires information on both, but should not contaminate one with the other when measuring skills. Therefore, measuring writing in more than one way is useful. Evaluation of the letter formation and spacing components of the motor execution task can be done by examining daily written work products, of course; but watching the youngster write in a controlled situation allows the teacher to note also the pencil grasp, left-to-right-progression, speed, and any unusual occurrences such as tremor.

The informal writing test begins by following again the general principle of testing downward. The more complex task of spontaneous writing to check language formulation and revisualization (memory) skills is presented first.

1. Provide the type of paper and pencil or pen used in the classroom.
2. Ask the student to write, in at least three sentences, three things that happened at school the day before. This provides a non-threatening content and is unlikely to be material the pupil has read or memorized.
3. Allow the pupil to write at his or her own rate without interruption. If the student asks for assistance, simply reply, "Do the best you can."
4. Ask the pupil to read aloud the sentences he or she has written. This will allow a check of self-corrections, since some learners will see errors and correct them by reading the accurate sentence instead of what has been written. If this happens, ask the youngster to make the correction in writing also.

Analysis of Formulation Errors

Analysis of formulation errors includes at least three factors, in addition to such formal elements as capitalization and punctuation which can be readily noted.

1. Syntax: Since word order is the basic element in English syntax, privilege-of-occurrence rules may be violated. That is, subject and object in a sentence may be re-

versed, adjectives may follow instead of preceding nouns, or subordinate clauses may be misplaced. The student may not write a sentence with a subject-predicate relationship, but may use fragments instead. In addition, critical function words such as articles, prepositions, or conjunctions may be omitted or used inappropriately.

2. Inflectional Markers: Inflections such as tense of verbs, number or possession on nouns, and comparative or superlative of adjectives which must be marked in standard English may be omitted by the student with language formulation problems.

3. Revisualization: Inadequate visual memory may lead to gross misspellings, omission of whole syllables from words, or substitution of a phonetically similar word.

If the spontaneous writing sample yields patterns of errors of syntax, inflections, or revisualization of words, the teacher has enough information to make some statements about the student's formulation skills. If, in addition, there is tremor or directional confusion or inadequate pencil grasp, these factors are important only if they result in inaccurate letter formation or spacing.

If both letter formation and spacing are comparable to the productions of other pupils in the class, the teacher need not proceed to test the motor component of writing. If, on the other hand, defects of letter formation or spacing occurred, or if letters were drawn in a slow, laborious process, the evaluation should proceed through an examination which will isolate motor execution from formulation.

1. Present a copying task, so that the student need not formulate the language nor revisualize the words.

2. Draw sentences to be copied from material at the student's independent or instructional reading level so that word recognition is not a variable. If the student has just completed the informal reading inventory, material should be drawn from passages read at 95% accuracy or above.

3. Construct a mask to cover most of the page so that a student who is visually distractible will not be penalized. Expose a passage of 12 to 20 words starting at the beginning of a sentence and ending with a period.
4. Ask the student to copy the passage from the book to a piece of paper on the desk in manuscript or cursive, depending upon grade level and the learner's exposure to instruction in cursive.
5. Tell the student to start and stop on your cue. Time the copying task for one minute, using a stopwatch. Consider every five letters as a word, regardless of the actual units in the passage, and compute the number of five-letter words copied in one minute.
6. Write a passage of comparable length, such as the next sentence on the page, on the chalkboard. Ask the student to copy from the board to a paper on the desk. Time for one minute using a stopwatch, and compute the number of five-letter words copied in one minute.

Analysis of Writing Errors

Analysis of errors in writing is not precise. Grade-level standards are not well established. Also, standards must be applied differently for manuscript and cursive writing, for right-handed and left-handed students, and in relation to posture, position of arm and wrist, orientation of paper on the desk, pencil grasp, visual acuity, and motor skills. Content, legibility, and fluency must be taken into account. Despite these variables, a few questions might be useful.

— How does performance on the copying task compare with that on the spontaneous writing sample? If the learner performed much better on the copying task in terms of letter formation and spacing, motor impairment is ruled out. If, however, defects occurred on the copying task as well as on the spontaneous sample, the problem may extend to motor execution.

— Does the learner use the same hand consistently for writing? A student aged 7 or above should have established a dominant hand for writing. If not, he or she should be observed in other activities for evidence of possible developmental lag in fine motor skills.

— What is the extent of directional confusion? If a few letters are reversed by a learner under the age of 9, there is no cause for concern. But if many letters or numerals are reversed, if sequencing of letters in a word proceeds from right to left, or if directionality is inconsistent, writing progress will be seriously affected.

— What is the relationship between speed and accuracy? If letters are adequately formed and spacing is conventional but rate is slow, there is less cause for concern than if letter formation or spacing is grossly inadequate but rate is fast. *Legibility should take precedence over speed.*

— What is the relationship of spacing between letters to spacing between words? If there is no difference or minimal difference, the learner may not be segmenting words properly, or may not realize that the word is a unit.

— What is the relationship between the quality of copying from the paper on the desk and copying from the board? If gross differences occur, the learner may be demonstrating near-point or far-point vision problems, or a perceptual problem characterized by inability to shift visual planes.

— Are all vowels formed in an imprecise manner so that *i* looks like *e*, and *o* and *a* are indistinguishable? This may be evidence of spelling problems. Older students who know they are not good spellers sometimes deliberately develop careless handwriting to disguise spelling errors.

— Is there any evidence of confusion of symbols such as numbers written in place of letters or vice versa? Such concept confusion can occur in either spontaneous writing or copying; it signals a failure to grasp the categories into which symbols are organized.

Informal Spelling Sample

While the spontaneous writing sample can provide some information about spelling skills, the fact that the vocabulary is not controlled in terms of word-recognition skills complicates interpretation. In other words, a student may fail to spell correctly on a spontaneous writing sample when attempting words which are not yet established in the reading vocabulary.

Although some students are good readers but weak spellers, the reverse (good spellers but weak readers) is less likely to occur. Reading and spelling have enough skills in common to permit an assumption that basic word-recognition skills contribute to accuracy in spelling. Any informal test of spelling skills should isolate spelling problems from word-recognition limitations. This is accomplished by using for spelling tests words known to be in the student's sight vocabulary, and suggests disregard of the adopted spelling text in favor of a teacher-constructed criterion test based on the results of the informal reading inventory. This recommendation is the only exception to the use of classroom texts in the teacher's diagnosis of academic skills.

In addition to isolating spelling problems as distinguished from word recognition problems, one must separate spelling from recall or memory factors and from impairments of motor execution. To accomplish this isolation, the same spelling words are presented in three ways—requiring the student's written, oral and multiple-choice response—employing the following steps:

1. Select 20 words which have been read successfully on the informal reading inventory. Words should be selected from the independent reading level, if it has been established. If not, items can be drawn from the words recognized correctly at the instructional reading level.
2. Selection should be made so that a variety of initial and final consonants, blends, and vowel combinations are represented. A balance also should be sought between

words which are phonetic for spelling and those which contain silent consonants or dipthongs. Approximately half the words selected should be those which are irregular in spelling or exceptions to spelling generalizations.

3. Pronounce each word orally and ask the student to write it spontaneously to your dictation. Place each word in a brief sentence so it has meaning for the student and possible homonyms are controlled. Repeat the stimulus word after reading the sentence.

4. As soon as the list of spelling words has been written, ask the student to check his or her own production as you re-read the stimulus words. Allow the student to make any spontaneous corrections by writing the word a second time immediately beside the first attempt. Offer no assistance during this self-correction.

5. Check the student's written production immediately. Ask him or her to spell orally any words misspelled in written form. Write the oral spelling beside the attempted spelling on the paper.

6. Print any stimulus words not spelled correctly, either in writing or orally, on 3″ x 5″ index cards. Print three distractor cards for each word, providing a minimal contrast by varying only a single letter or at the most two letters from the correct spelling of the stimulus word.

7. Spread out the four cards for each stimulus word in random fashion. Read the stimulus word aloud and ask the student to point to the correct spelling on one of the four cards.

8. If alphabetizing skills are to be assessed, the distractor cards prepared for the previous step can be presented to examine the student's ability to arrange four cards on the basis of second, third, or fourth letters in the word.

Analysis of Spelling Errors

Error analysis in spelling begins with comparing performance on the three methods of response (written, oral, and multiple-choice) to spelling tasks. If the student could write 90% of the words spontaneously to oral dictation, he or she has demonstrated adequate spelling skills. If oral spelling and the multiple-choice task were required, these questions should be asked:

— What is the relationship between words spelled correctly in written form to dictation and those spelled orally? If more words can be spelled orally than in writing, problems in revisualization or motor execution are suspect. Examination of the writing sample will provide additional evidence to establish the nature of the problem.

— What is the relationship between words spelled correctly by selection from four choices and words spelled orally? If more words can be selected by multiple choice than can be spelled spontaneously, the learner may be demonstrating recall problems. However, the difference must be substantial before memory disorder is suspected, since a high rate of correct response by chance is present in any multiple-choice tasks.

Errors in written or oral spelling should be analyzed to establish patterns by answering questions such as:

— Are letter substitutions related to *auditory* similarity, as *t* for *k*, or to *visual* similarity, such as *b* for *h*? Implications for the first might include a check of hearing acuity if the error is frequent. For the visual similarity, a check of letter formation might reveal some confusion unrelated to spelling, or the apparent substitution may be accounted for by careless penmanship.

— Do responses indicate that spelling generalizations may not have been taught? A student who consistently writes *haveing* or *crys* or *carefuly* may not have been exposed to rules for adding inflections or doubling of consonants.

— Do responses suggest overreliance on auditory cues, such as *shur* for *sure*, or *lisen* for *listen*? Are vowel substitutions phonetic, such as *upropriut* for *appropriate*? Such errors are evidence of problems with revisualization or visual memory.

— Are spelling errors related to articulation problems, such as substitution of *w* for *r* or *l* or gross mispronunciations in speech, such as *gaspet* for *basket?*

— Are errors consistent with dialect pronunciations such as *skreet* for *street, hep* for *help,* or *court* for *caught.* If the student is a dialect speaker, differences in sound patterns in the dialect must not be confused with spelling errors.

— What is the relationship between the spelling perform-ance and the vocabulary items on the reading comprehension test? Lack of knowledge of word meanings can account for inadequate spelling performance because the task becomes rote memorization of meaningless material.

— Do substitutions fit a consistent pattern or are they random? Application of rules to spelling may be an indication of strength even though the rules are misapplied or over-generalized. A learner who spells according to phonics generali-zations, for example, will be accurate only about half the time, but the student demonstrates the ability to apply deductive rea-soning to the academic task, and can seek out a strategy for solving a problem. The student whose errors are random, on the other hand, exhibits inability to marshall learning strategies, and the prognosis for remediation is guarded.

— What is the percentage of self-corrections? A high pro-portion of spontaneously corrected words indicates strength in monitoring performance even though skills are not at the auto-matic level. Spoiling a correct response or adding a second incorrect response is evidence that the first spelling is not estab-lished in the student's repertoire and could be readily extinguished.

These suggestions for informal classroom inventories re-quire a considerable amount of preparation the first time they are undertaken. However, material prepared for the informal samples can be used again and again, as long as adopted texts remain the same. In addition, teachers in the same building could easily divide preparation of reading and math materials and share them on a staggered testing schedule.

3

Referral

Some referrals may be made *before* the teacher has completed the Diagnostic stage, if the evidence warrants immediate evaluation by support personnel. When diagnostic testing is completed, the teacher is in a position to make decisions about which of the remaining students with potentially handicapping conditions should be referred for additional diagnostic work by fellow professionals preparatory to development of the individualized education program.

A few students may be considered for trial classroom intervention prior to referral. In general, these learners will be those whose levels of academic functioning are less than two years below the average for the class. Their social skills will be at age-appropriate levels; or the teacher should be able to identify specific interfering behaviors or situational factors which lead to a belief that environmental or motivational changes might have an immediate effect on skills performance. This group will be managed by the classroom teacher for a period of time while he or she observes progress and determines whether additional referrals are indicated. The remaining students who have been subjected to intensive academic diagnosis will be referred to support personnel.

Students classified in the referral group will fit a variety of patterns. The characteristics revealed by each student at the Identification and Diagnosis stages must be reviewed by the teacher in order to make decisions about appropriate sources for referral. For the teacher in the public school, the referral sources to be considered first are those within the school district. A list of available services should be obtained from the building principal, or information can be gained at inservice programs conducted by support personnel in the district. Because a teacher usually makes referrals through the building principal, the teacher and the principal must have a working agreement about the referral procedures to be followed and the presenting problems which will be considered appropriate for referral.

A conference with the principal at the beginning of the year should establish the procedures by which to request assistance from support persons. Any forms which must be completed by the teacher should be obtained at this time. If the referral form must be reviewed by a screening committee at the building level before it is sent to another level, the teacher must know the contact person for that committee and the schedule of screening meetings. The teacher also should discuss at the outset the arrangements which the principal is willing to make to free the teacher from the classroom in order to be available for screening meetings. On this point, the teacher must be prepared to assert the right and obligation to provide direct information when decisions are being made about evaluating one of his or her students. Omission of teacher information should not be justified on the basis of lack of coverage of the class, since discussion of a given pupil may require no more than 20 minutes at the screening level, and supervision should be possible for that period of time.

Although the decision about which support person is to evaluate a student will seldom be made by the teacher alone, the available resources may be clearly examined if they are classified into three levels of assessment — Academic Functioning Level, Process Functioning Level, and Cognitive/Affective Functioning Level. Sources of professional consultation and considerations for referral differ at each level.

ACADEMIC FUNCTIONING LEVEL

At the most obvious level of description, the Academic Functioning Level, a learner's status in regard to basic skills of reading, mathematics, writing, and spelling is identified, as is achievement across classroom curriculum areas. At this level, the most appropriate person to conduct the evaluation is the classroom teacher. Indeed, the procedures described in the previous section on Diagnosis could be expected to yield precise descriptions of academic strengths and weaknesses. The teacher's assessment at this level is more reliable than that of support personnel because of the direct contact with the pupil over time, which allows assessment based upon almost unlimited samples of the academic behavior in question.

In contrast, some support personnel who might engage in assessment at the Academic Functioning Level operate at a disadvantage. Because they can allocate only a specific period of time for testing, they must use screening measures of achievement rather than diagnostic instruments. Furthermore, typical school psychologists and counselors are not curriculum specialists; they are not trained in scope and sequence of content or skills, and they are seldom in a position to isolate specific skills in academic areas. Even if such an examiner is an experienced classroom teacher, the achievement information is only a small portion of the battery which must be presented, so precise diagnostic academic information is not likely to result from testing by psychologists or counselors. However, referral at this level may be appropriate if other specialists, such as the following, are available.

The Special Educator

Special educators who serve in the role of resource room or learning center teachers or itinerant methods and materials consultants can provide help to the regular classroom teacher at the Academic Functioning Level. A special teacher may have certification in mental retardation, learning disabilities, emotional disturbance, or some combination of two of these certifications. Such a teacher may hold a Master's degree and may be trained to administer batteries of informal skills tests and standardized individual tests of achievement. This teacher typically schedules his or her workload so as to spend the first four weeks or so of each school term testing learners who were referred the previous spring, then retains one-half day each week to test additional students who are referred during the school year. Although the caseload which a resource room or itinerant teacher can carry is specified by state guidelines, more turnover occurs in this type of program than in the self-contained classroom, so that most special educators in these roles can accept referrals throughout the school year.

Referral to the resource room, learning center, or itinerant teacher for assessment is indicated if the teacher's own classroom methods have not yielded information specific enough to be used for individual academic programming. The classroom teacher might refer for assistance with one skills area, such as arithmetic or writing, after exhausting the evaluation procedures in his or her own repertoire. The special educator who works with wide variations in skills performance is able to establish detailed academic strengths and weaknesses.

The Subject-Matter Specialist

Another person who might be consulted at the Academic Functioning Level is the special reading teacher, who might be asked to administer an individual skills test or to conduct trial teaching to discover why a given student is not responding to reading instruction. The special reading teacher has diagnosic instruments which can build upon the informal reading inventory to yield more precise information for programming.

For assistance at this level of assessment, the curriculum supervisor for mathematics or language arts might also be consulted to recommend specific methods or materials to investigate an instructional problem. Such supervisors do not usually conduct evaluations themselves, but they may be able to suggest classroom methods of assessment which the teacher has not considered. With these exceptions, *the Academic Functioning Level is the province of the classroom teacher.*

PROCESS FUNCTIONING LEVEL

At the second level of description, which can be called the Process Functioning Level, sensory acuity is checked, physical health is evaluated, and many of the perceptual and expressive subskills which are presumed to underlie academic skills can be inferred. An experienced clinician can draw inferences about the student's strengths and weaknesses in terms of processes which cannot be directly observed, are difficult to isolate due to confounding or overlapping of task dimensions, or involve psychological constructs which are difficult to validate. Such an evaluation requires a battery of tests. As there is generally some degree of overlap of indicators in different tests, the presence of a single indicator provides the basis for a hypothesis which is then confirmed or disconfirmed by further measures. *Testing at the second level of assessment is the province of the specially trained clinician.*

Many professional persons are potential referral resources at the second level of assessment. *School district resources* available in most districts include the school nurse, the speech clinician, the educational diagnostician, the school psychologist or the counselor; other personnel such as hearing conservationists, social workers, or consulting psychologists are available in some districts. *Community resources* include the clinical audiologist, the physical therapist, the occupational therapist, and medical personnel such as the pediatrician. Channels for referral are dictated by district policy, and any referral to community resources typically is handled by consultation among the parents, the principal, and possibly the school nurse. Examples of indications for referral to some of these specialists may clarify referral decisions. Because role descriptions for these experts vary according to district guidelines and state licensure, the examples are suggestive rather than definitive.

The Nurse

Teachers are not always alerted to the fact that chronic or recurring health problems can be as handicapping as any of the traditional categories of exceptionality. Students with allergies, for example, may miss a great deal of instruction due to temporary hearing loss which occurs when inflammation blocks the passages which ventilate the middle ear. If a pupil appears to have chronic upper respiratory problems, nasal drainage, or a cough, he or she may have allergies. Another health problem, diabetes, is a possibility if a student is chronically thirsty, asks to go to the bathroom frequently, and eats large lunches and snacks but doesn't seem to gain weight. If this student sometimes complains of blurred vision or cramps in the legs or abdomen, action should be taken immediately to secure a medical examination.

A condition which may be misjudged in the classroom as a behavioral habit rather than a medical problem is the petit mal seizure, usually characterized by brief spells of "staring" which may seem to be mere woolgathering. The pupil may blink rapidly between periods of staring, or may turn aside and appear to "tune out" the environment. Because these seizures do not cause loss of consciousness or even change of position, the student is able to resume academic work as if nothing had happened. But something *has* happened—part of the lesson has been missed. If seizure activity is frequent, a student can miss essential instruction over time.

Numerous other health problems require referral to the nurse. Excessive fatigue may signal cardiac problems or severe anemia. A primary pupil who squirms frequently may have pinworms. A youngster with poor hygiene and a general appearance of neglect may also be malnourished. In addition to symptoms of impaired health, questions of development should also be referred first to the school nurse, who will make further referrals if necessary.

The highest priority for referral to the nurse should be those students who demonstrate possible vision or hearing disorders. Because many youngsters experience reading and other learning problems due to faulty vision, or cannot cope with classroom instructions and language in general because of mild hearing loss, identification of students whose behavior indicates the need for vision or hearing evaluation can offer a straightforward solution for many academic problems.

Behavior which should lead a teacher to suspect a defect in vision would include any unusual appearance or positioning of the eyes or atypical positioning of the head when looking at visual stimuli. Other behaviors to be noted are covering one eye while reading or looking at the blackboard; moving a paper or book back and forth in the line of vision as if to bring it into focus; persistent rubbing of the eyes; closing eyes or resting forehead on arm frequently while reading; jerking or quick movement of the pupil of the eye; complaints of eye fatigue, double or blurred vision, or chronic headaches.

Behavioral symptoms of possible hearing loss might include complaints of pain, or persistent tugging or rubbing of an ear; turning the head toward the direction of sound; lack of response to speech originating behind the learner; unusually close attention to the mouth of a speaker; requests for repetition of instructions when conditions are noisy or the pupil is farther from the teacher than usual; severe articulation problems, including omission of many consonant sounds; lack of response to phonics instruction despite adequate teaching with a variety of methods over a period of time. Many of these symptoms are likely to be displayed by pupils with chronic and severe throat

79

and upper respiratory infections, asthma, or allergies affecting the respiratory system. The nurse should be the first resource for referral for questions of hearing impairment, but the nurse may in turn refer the student for evaluation by others in the district who may be qualified to test hearing.

The Speech Clinician

The speech and language clinician has had some course work in audiology and may be able to obtain an air conduction threshold to establish the minimum loudness level at which a student could be expected to interpret sounds accurately. The equipment used in a school is not as accurate as that in a clinic, of course, but the speech clinician may be able to determine more carefully whether the student requires referral to a community clinic or hospital than can the school nurse, who often conducts only a sweep check at a single loudness level across sound frequencies.

The role of the speech clinician in the public school is expanding to include evaluation and treatment of disorders of language or concept development, rather than being limited to disorders of articulation, voice, or fluency. A student should be referred if he or she demonstrates language usage which frequently confuses word order, as in, "The cat I put outside," or usage which appears to be that of a chronologically younger child, such as, "Him sat down" or "He goed" from an 8-year-old student. Indications of memory lapse or word-finding problems, such as saying, "The thing you sit in," instead of "chair," may be cause for referral if they are reliable in the pupil's language. Echolalia—repetition of the exact words of another person instead of a response—should always be cause for referral. If consonant substitutions, omissions, or distortions make speech unintelligible or if they distract from the content of the message, articulation testing is indicated.

All children are relatively dysfluent, and a student who seems to stutter under the stress of classroom question and answer sessions is not necessarily a stutterer. But the student should be evaluated if he or she chronically repeats initial sounds or syllables, prolongs words, or blocks repeatedly, or if dysfluency is accompanied by secondary symptoms such as associated movements of arms, legs, head, or facial grimace.

The Educational Diagnostician

The diagnostician usually is an experienced special educator who has spent considerable time in classroom teaching of exceptional students, then qualified through additional course work and field experiences to become an expert at educational diagnosis. The diagnostician can conduct both formal and informal evaluation of skills, but also can explore the perceptual and expressive subskills which are presumed to underlie academic functioning. If such a person is available, referral to the diagnostician might be considered as an alternative to, or prior to, referral to a school psychologist or counselor. Indications for referral to the diagnostician include stubborn instructional problems which have not yielded to modification of materials, such as the youngster whose hearing is intact but who does not respond to phonics instruction, or the student whose academic performance is so inconsistent that mastery levels cannot be established.

The typical diagnostician is not certified to administer individual measures of intelligence, but usually is trained to administer most of the same standardized tests as the school psychologist or counselor. However, the diagnostician is more likely to use informal approaches to measure the youngster's subskills or preferred learning modality. He or she may present the same task in two or three different ways, for example, to learn which method produces the best results when the youngster is retested an hour later.

The School Psychologist or Counselor

Although their roles in terms of services vary considerably, assessment roles of the school psychologist and counselor may include the same tests at the Process Level. Typically, they administer tests of visual and auditory perception and fine-motor skills. The area in which these two specialists can offer the greatest assistance at the second level of assessment is probably in their ability to describe the student's learning style or problem-solving approaches.

Because of training and experience with a wide variety of tests and procedures, they are able to conduct refined analyses of interactions of subtest scores and even individual items on tests. Such analyses make it possible to amass evidence to state that a given student is primarily a visual learner, for example, or that his or her strength lies in processing of verbal information rather than manual tasks. Their training allows these specialists to draw inferences about psychological constructs which are not directly measurable and are difficult to validate.

Referral to a school psychologist or counselor for Process Level assessment is indicated if the teacher has observational data to support a suspicion that a student demonstrates a specific severe perceptual or expressive deficit; if the teacher cannot program successfully for the student without information on his or her most favorable learning style; if the youngster is failing to profit from classroom instruction which emphasizes a specific modality (such as a strongly phonics-oriented basal reader).

A referral for Process Level evaluation by a counselor or school psychologist is not indicated if the teacher is merely curious to learn whether the student may demonstrate some type of "learning disability." *The referral is appropriate only if it is determined to be necessary to answer a specific presenting problem.* Vague, undefined suggestions of possible perceptual or motor problems are not cause for referral if these possible problems do not interfere with academic work or if the teacher is able to program effectively for the pupil in spite of the problem.

Because many teachers lack confidence in their ability to develop an appropriate program for an exceptional student, they make many referrals for Process Level testing which may be unnecessary. For example, if third-grader Johnny has not mastered manuscript printing, the teacher has an instructional problem, and may determine that referral is indicated to ascertain whether a fine-motor lag may be responsible. But the psychologist's tests, which establish that Johnny indeed demonstrates a developmental lag in visual-motor integration, do not tell the teacher how to solve the instructional problem any more than do the teacher's own observations of Johnny's attempts to write his name. In fact, the name-writing task, which is closer to the terminal behavior, is likely to yield more useful information than the student's reproduction of geometric forms on the psychologist's tests. Referral for Process Level testing should be considered only if the teacher cannot program for the student without it, and only if the teacher can specify a presenting problem which must be answered in order to instruct the pupil.

The Clinical Audiologist

After school district resources for hearing evaluation have been exhausted, a referral to a clinical audiologist may be considered if the nurse or the speech clinician suspects an undiagnosed hearing impairment. Working in a sound-treated room with carefully calibrated equipment, the clinical audiologist can go beyond the identification of hearing impairment to quantify the loss, follow air conduction testing with bone conduction and discrimination testing, determine whether refer ral to an otologist (physician who treats the ear) is indicated for medical or surgical treatment, or recommend an aid if appropriate. Indications for referral to an audiologist may be any of those mentioned as cause for referral to the nurse; a teacher seldom refers directly to a clinical audiologist without consulting personnel within the district.

The Physical Therapist

If a student demonstrates a physical handicap affecting gross motor movements, the physical therapist can be of assistance in diagnosing specific areas for intervention. Frequently, the physical therapist works in consultation with the physical education instructor to design an adapted program for gross motor development or to provide the exercise a student might need. Since basic gross motor skills should be established by the age of 6, deviations from normal development tend to be rather obvious in the school-age population. A student may demonstrate an awkward gait, walk on tiptoe, or appear uncoordinated in playground or gym games. A teacher may notice that a student does not seem to have protective reflexes such as extending the arms to break a fall or crossing one leg over the other to right the body when losing balance sideward. If a pupil cannot go up and down stairs with alternating feet, or skip with alternating feet, or can't throw a ball overhand with accurate placement, or if one side of the body seems to be working in opposition rather than in cooperation with the other side, there may be cause for concern.

Of course, all children and adolescents are awkward at times, and this behavior does not interfere with academic or social development. But if the teacher has reason to suspect undiagnosed gross motor problems, the nurse should be consulted about possible referral to a physical therapist for testing of higher level reflexes and gross motor development.

The Occupational Therapist

The occupational therapist is concerned with assessment of fine-motor skills, especially those associated with hand movements such as buttoning, tying, zipping, and other self-help skills. Because one of the basic tools for classroom work is writing, problems in fine-motor development can have many implications for academic failure.

A major skill which a youngster must develop in order to write is proper pencil grasp, with the pencil between the tip of the thumb and index finger resting against the side of the middle finger. A pupil who still uses a palmar grasp may be demonstrating a developmental lag. By the age of 6, a child should have established hand preference and should be able to write or copy in a left-to-right progression. He or she should be able to use a scissors, lace and tie shoes, and use classroom tools such as a crank pencil sharpener. If a youngster has reached the age of 7 or 8 without these skills and is not functioning adequately in written work, consultation with the nurse should be sought to determine whether evaluation of fine-motor skills should be considered.

These examples of school and community resources available for Process Level assessment are not exhaustive. Teachers in a metropolitan community may have access to additional sources of diagnostic information at this level.

COGNITIVE AND AFFECTIVE FUNCTIONING LEVEL

The third level of assessment could be called the Cognitive and Affective Functioning Level. Thinking strategies and emotional status are separate factors, of course, but they are combined for discussion because they interact to some extent and because individually administered tests which measure intellectual functioning can also be interpreted to reveal personality characteristics and feeling states. *Tests designed to measure intellectual and affective characteristics of a student in a school setting are reserved to experts who undergo special training* under supervision, and who are bound by strict ethics in the administration and interpretation of tests.

The School Psychologist and the Counselor

Because the assessment roles assumed by the psychologist and the counselor in a school setting differ from district to district depending upon the availability of other personnel with psychometric training, their roles will not be distinguished here. Typically, both are certified to administer and interpret three or four individual tests of intellectual functioning, measures of personality such as sentence completion tasks, projective tests, or self-reporting scales, aptitude tests, and interest inventories.

If placement of a student in a special class or in a resource room for part of a day is proposed, the school psychologist or counselor must be involved in the assessment. Although additional data are considered, placement of a student in special services typically requires evaluation of intellectual functioning level and social-emotional status.

Indications for Referral

Indications for referral to establish intellectual functioning level include both academic and social behaviors. Behaviors revealed in the classroom which should lead to referral include those of a student who requires an unusual number of trials to master an arithmetic operation easily grasped by most of the class; a pupil who is unable to remember on Tuesday a concept seemingly learned on Monday; a youngster whose independent work is done slowly with numerous errors which he or she cannot self-correct. Some characteristics assume more importance as the youngster reaches intermediate grades. If the learner at this level still demonstrates language or speech patterns of a younger child, doesn't know what year, month, or day of the week it is, can't read a clock face, or tends to get lost in the building on the way to the principal's office or the gym, this student may be a candidate for evaluation of intellectual functioning.

Social indicators for evaluation of intellectual functioning include a preference for chronologically younger playmates, and/or inadequate social judgment as in asking personal questions of teachers or failing to pick up cues for behavior by watching older students or adults. Another reason to refer for evaluation of intellectual functioning level would be some evidence that the youngster does not seem to know the difference between dealing with a stranger or a friend, in that normal reticence may be missing or familiarity too quickly established.

Referral for evaluation of intellectual functioning level is not indicated simply because the teacher does not know the learner's intelligence quotient. If a student enters a classroom without a group or individual IQ on record, the teacher should be able to plan appropriately on the basis of classroom behavior and response to instruction. Only if apparent discrepancies exist between estimated IQ and achievement, or if extremely high or extremely low functioning is suspected, is the IQ essential for purposes of planning by the classroom teacher.

Behavioral indications for referral to assess emotional states may be demonstrated in the classroom or on the playground: the student who typically withdraws from peer and teacher contact or is unresponsive to offers to participate in games or other activities; the pupil who chronically lashes out verbally or motorically in an impulsive way, will not wait in line or take turns, cries or throws objects when thwarted, or overreacts to minor slights or setbacks and does not change these behaviors when the teacher imposes limits or rewards appropriate behavior; the youngster who engages in cruel or aggressive acts against other students, animals, or the property of others without re- morse; the student who frequently complains of vague physical illnesses and uses such complaints to avoid classroom tasks; the youngster who engages in ritualistic self-stimulating activity.

Some of the above behaviors may be demonstrated when a pupil is under stress of some situational disturbance, such as his parents' impending divorce or the loss of a parent or sibling through death, or even the minor adjustment of moving the family's residence. If the situation is known to the teacher and if social behavior seems to change in relation to the situation, the student probably need not be referred for evaluation. Another professional's agreeing that the youngster is indeed reacting to stress will not be of further help; the student will still have to adjust to the situation. Instead of referring for assessment, consultation might be sought to learn ways to smooth the student's course.

On the other hand, some of these behaviors might occur in reaction to the situational stress of physical or psychological battering. In such a case, the teacher's responsibility is much greater, and other professionals should be brought into the case as soon as battering is suspected so that documentation can be collected according to state law.

ESSENTIAL STEPS IN REFERRAL

When appropriate resources for referral to specialists have been identified, the teacher must do four things:

1. Communicate the student's status according to results of classrom testing and observation;
2. Report any interventions which have been attempted and any token economy or incentive systems in use in the classroom;
3. Ask specific referral questions to be answered by the specialists who will conduct the evaluation; and
4. Prepare the student for referral.

Communication of Student Status

In some districts, referral for testing by specialists is initiated by completing a written referral form. A form offers the advantage of securing the exact information required by the specialist, but it is seldom comprehensive enough to permit the teacher who has conducted his or her own diagnostic testing to communicate all pertinent information about a pupil.

All relevant information known to the teacher must be shared with the specialist. If this is not done, the testing may not go beyond what the teacher already knows about the student, and valuable time will have been lost in retracing ground already explored by the teacher. Totally inappropriate, for example, is a teacher's referral for evaluation of visual or auditory processes involved in a reading task without simultaneously reporting the student's instructional reading level, scores on skills tests in word recognition and comprehension, and the student's level of vocabulary and grammar. If a teacher refers a student as a reading problem without sharing this information, the specialist will have to spend a great deal of the available testing time to establish this information. Instead, the specialist should go beyond skills information to examine subskills, but the teacher must make that possible by sharing all he or she knows at the time of referral.

If a referral form is used in the district, it can be completed as required, and supplemented by a narrative presentation of additional information yielded by classroom methods.

If the information is to be communicated at a building screening meeting, or at the IEP conference, the data usually are presented orally. An oral report must be succinct and must be very clearly stated, since the listeners have no opportunity to look back for figures as might be possible when the information is written. Statements must be brief sentences, organized to emphasize points the teacher believes are most important. Numbers, which are difficult to remember if heard only once, are to be repeated or paraphrased in a summary statement at the end.

A typical organization of data might be as follows:

1. Current grade levels in reading recognition and comprehension, mathematics computation and reasoning, spelling, and writing.
2. Major skills deficits which account for discrepancies in any of the grade level relationships.
3. Behavioral characteristics which might interfere with academic work.
4. Restatement of grade levels or discrepancies; restatement of strengths.

An example of such a series of statements is seen in the brief report of the status of third-grade student Jim.

Jim's instructional reading level is preprimer. Arithmetic skills are generally at low second-grade level. Spelling is at a low first-grade level. Manuscript writing rate scores at first-grade level.

Addition and subtraction are accurate but problems are written with directional reversals. Arithmetic computation skills are stronger than reasoning skills because Jim cannot read word problems in the text. However, he understands the materials if they are read to him, so he has the vocabulary and sentence structure to read third-grade materials if he could decode them. Word recognition deficits occur in consonant blends and medial vowels. Sight vocabulary is not reliable. Spelling errors are chiefly medial vowel substitutions which are phonetically based. Writing rate is affected by reversals of letter forms and by interfering behaviors such as repeatedly dropping a pencil or eraser and taking considerable time to retrieve them.

> Other interfering behaviors include staring into space for periods up to one minute, and placing his head on the desk with eyes closed when he should be working. Jim is a slow-moving, passive youngster who causes no trouble but makes no academic progress. He seems bright because he understands so much of what is read to him; left to himself, however, he does not stay on task and completes no work.
>
> Since Jim is in the second half of third grade, his math grade level is 1½ years behind, his instructional reading level is fully three years behind, and spelling and writing are two years behind the average. Strengths are demonstrated in comprehension of oral language, some understanding of phonics, and reliable computation skills in addition and subtraction.

This type of oral report takes only a few minutes to present, yet offers considerable information of use to someone else who will be asked to evaluate the youngster. If the report is written, some qualifying information can be added, sentences can be more varied, and the summary is probably not necessary. However, the information should still be presented in a straightforward way, without attempts at interpretation.

Report of Interventions and Economy Systems

The oral or written report of the status of a student in regard to academic skills should always be accompanied by information about interventions which the teacher has already attempted. Any special materials or methods which have been presented, and the length of time they have been applied, should be mentioned. Interventions should be reported whether they were successful or not—the potential examiner must know what the student has been exposed to and how he or she has reacted. If this information is not presented, the teacher may find that the examiner might recommend an intervention which has already been attempted unsuccessfully. In the case of Jim, for example, the teacher might say:

> A word family, or consonant-substitution method of teaching sight words was attempted in an effort to draw attention to the medial vowel. Jim performed well on the (name) materials over an eight-week period, but he did not transfer the skills to the basal text.

If any type of token economy or structured reward system is in use in the classroom, the potential examiner must have this information in order to incorporate it into any recommendation which might result from testing. The teacher might say of Jim, for example:

> A token system in the classroom allows the youngsters to earn points for appropriate task behaviors. For six weeks Jim was offered five points for every page of seatwork completed; he could use the points at the end of the day to purchase a game to play or to listen to a record. For the first two weeks he earned about 10 points a day; since then he has averaged only about 15 points over a week, even though I have varied the activities he could buy.

Formulation of the Referral Question

As the person who initiated the referral, the teacher is in a position of having to justify it. This can be done only by demonstrating (a) that certain questions about the student must be answered if instruction is to be planned, and (b) that such questions cannot be answered by classroom procedures. The referral question is not an esoteric statement understood only by a psychometrist. Instead, it is simply a straightforward question specifying what the teacher must know in order to program effectively for the student. Some guidelines in formulating the question might be helpful in soliciting useful data.

First, *the question should be answerable*—it must be one which is subject to analysis of observable behavior or inferences drawn from observable behavior. It should not probe the causes of behavior, which may not be answerable. For example, instead of asking, "Does Jim's passivity indicate emotional causes for lack of achievement?" a more useful question might be, "What might motivate Jim to complete work independently in the classroom?"

Second, *the question should be as precise as the teacher can state it*—it should be specific enough to permit the examiner to answer it with detailed information instead of generalities. Instead of asking, for example, "Does Jim seem to be a learning disabled child?" which might require the examiner to reflect on *all* the behavioral characteristics of learning disabilities, the teacher might ask, "Do Jim's apparent visual deficits constitute a learning disability?"

Third, *the question should derive directly from what is already known about the student.* Since, in Jim's case, there are no known behavioral indicators of hearing impairment, phonics skills are among the student's strengths, and he retains and comprehends much of what is read to him or what he hears on tape or on records, the teacher has no reason to ask for the routine hearing evaluation which might be appropriate for most disabled readers who do not demonstrate Jim's characteristics.

Instead, the evidence from observation and classroom testing would support a vision screening, compatible with symptoms of eye fatigue, confusion of letter forms, and phonetic spelling. The low energy level, lack of productivity, and symptoms of fatigue also would support a referral for medical examination to verify or rule out physical causes for failure to achieve. The question should be formulated to answer presenting problems for Jim as an individual who has been described by the teacher as precisely as classroom methods will allow, but who still is not evaluated thoroughly enough to permit immediate programming for academic skills.

Referral questions should be stated at the end of the status report, after any attempted interventions or motivation systems have been described. The teacher might want to ask about Jim:

> Are there medical or physical reasons for slow movements, lack of energy, and low classroom productivity? Is visual acuity adequate for making discriminations among similar letters such as *a, e,* and *o?* Do visual memory deficits in spelling, spatial disorganization in computing problems, and lack of sight vocabulary constitute a specific visual disability? Does Jim need special reading techniques? Or should insistence on reading give way to alternative kinds of instruction? What motivational strategies are suggested by Jim's test behavior?

Preparation of the Student for Referral

If the results of testing conducted by professional specialists are to be valid and useful, testing must be conducted under optimal conditions. Factors which affect test results include the appropriateness of the testing room, the examiner's ability to establish rapport, and freedom from distractions which could interfere with attention and concentration on test tasks. These factors frequently become problems in crowded, noisy school buildings when the counselor or school psychologist feels pressed to move as quickly as possible through a heavy caseload of referrals. But these are conditions beyond the control of the classroom teacher; the responsibility lies with administrative and special services personnel. However, one factor over which the teacher does have control is preparation of the student for referral. Some clinicians greet a youngster at the beginning of a testing session by asking, "Do you know why you are here?" Any experienced clinician can testify that too frequently students are bewildered at finding themselves in the presence of a stranger, unaware of what will be done or what demands will be placed upon them, anxious about what may be wrong with them to lead to such a circumstance, and resentful of the adults who placed them in this position against their will.

If a student is to be motivated to cooperate with testing, four types of information must be conveyed at the time he or she is told that evaluation is to take place. The statements a teacher makes should answer the questions which are likely to be on the student's mind. The question, "Why are you doing this?" is answered by describing the purpose of the testing. "What will I have to do?" can be answered by a brief, general overview of probable procedures. "Will I find out how I did?" is met with an assurance that the student will receive feedback about the test performance. The question, "What will happen after the testing?" can be answered by describing the staffing procedure and the planning of a program.

Statement of Purpose

Regardless of the student's age, he or she deserves to know why the teacher thinks an evaluation is necessary. As soon as parental permission for testing has been secured, a pupil aged 9 or above can be told what is to happen. For primary children, the teacher would be wise to wait until the first appointment is imminent. A simple, straightforward statement is best. A teacher might say, for example, "Jim, you know we've had trouble finding the right books for you to use so you can do good work. We've done as much as we can in the class, and now I want to ask Mrs. Smith to help us by giving you some tests."

Regardless of the wording, the message should include specific points:

1. The problem is acknowledged. No point is gained in glossing over the fact that the student is in trouble academically — the student knows he or she is not succeeding. Often the teacher's frank statement acknowledging a problem allows the student to admit it to himself or herself for the first time — a necessary step to solving any problem.
2. No blame is being assigned. The positive step of attempting a solution is emphasized, rather than the negative aspects of fault. This should reassure the student that recognizing a difficulty need not be associated with guilt.
3. The person who will conduct the testing is a *helper*. This statement should avoid the possibility of the student's viewing the examiner as a threatening figure with some type of power over the student.

Description of Procedures

A positive work set prior to testing can be established if students know something about the demands which will be placed upon them. If the evaluation is to include medical testing, the teacher may want to solicit the help of the nurse to explain what will be done. If testing is to be done by the school psychologist or the counselor, a simple and general explanation should suffice. Even if a teacher knows exactly which tests will be in the battery (which he or she probably does not) a precise description of testing tasks would invalidate any test. Instead, the pupil might be told, for example, "You will answer some questions, probably use a pencil and paper, and maybe put some things together with your hands. Some of the work will be like what you do in school. Some will be different. Some will be easy, and some will be harder. Just do the very best you can."

The points to be conveyed are these:

1. This will be work, not play. Some teachers make the mistake of leading the student to expect games, and the student is justifiably resentful when the tasks turn out to be difficult. The student must understand that the undertaking is serious.
2. Some unfamiliar tasks may be presented. This allows the student time to prepare for some flexibility in adapting to the demands of the tasks, and it lets the student know that he or she will not be expected to recognize everything which is presented.
3. Some of the work will be difficult. Again, a realistic picture of the test should be conveyed so the student will not become upset upon reaching his or her ceiling.
4. The student's best efforts will be required, but best is good enough.

Guarantee of Feedback

The issue of providing feedback to a student, concerning performance in evaluations by other professionals, goes to the very heart of the educational process. The teacher who views learning as a cooperative venture with responsibility shared equally by student and guide will have no difficulty discussing test results with the pupil. The teacher who views the task as that of directing outcomes from a position of authority with the responsibility squarely on the teacher's shoulders may see little reason to convey test results to the student. A teacher who has been accustomed to sharing test results with administrators and parents but not with the testee will have some adjustments to make.

Results must be reported in language the student can understand. Even a first-grade child can grasp the results at some level. However, all professionals must be careful to avoid use of technical or emotion-laden terms which may raise, rather than alleviate, anxiety. The teacher might say, "Mrs. Smith will tell us what you do best, and what is hardest for you. You and I will look at what you did and what it means in the classroom." The information to be conveyed is this:

1. The teacher is looking for what the student *can* do as well as what he or she cannot do well.
2. The student is a partner, and has equal access to the data.
3. The results will be interpreted in terms of what goes on in the classroom.

Description of Outcomes

The student deserves to know how the test results will be used, but the teacher probably does not need to go beyond the description of the staffing process. Since the teacher has no way of predicting any outcomes beyond the staffing, he or she would be overstepping the teacher role by attempting to explain possible options. In the case of a placement question, for example, the teacher has no reason to anticipate the test results by telling a student that he or she might be removed from the room—this is entirely too anxiety-provoking and quite unnecessary. Rather, a teacher might say, "When the tests are finished, all the people who tested you will meet with me to talk about what we can do to help you. We will probably want to do some things we haven't done before, but we will talk them over with you and your parents first." The information to be presented to the student is this:

1. No single person will make a decision.
2. The discussion will center on how to help the student.
3. *Some* changes in the student's routine will be forthcoming.
4. The student and his or her parents will be consulted before those changes are made.

Preparing a student for testing by other professionals is one small facet of the teacher's comprehensive task of making the student a full partner in the educational process. By enlisting the student's cooperation at every stage of the referral process, the teacher guides the student through a series of joint decisions toward a mutual goal.

4

The Assessment Team

After the student has been evaluated by appropriate professional specialists, a staffing conference usually is the next step in the procedures. In compliance with the Education for All Handicapped Children Act of 1975 (PL 94-142), persons who are required to participate in the development of the individualized education program should be present at the IEP planning conference. This group should include a representative of the school (usually the principal or a special services administrator), the parent, guardian, or surrogate parent, the student, the teacher, and at least one member of the evaluation team, usually the school psychologist.

Several aspects of PL 94-142 can be interpreted as resulting in increased participation of the classroom teacher:

1. The requirement that parents be involved directly in developing the individualized education program means that conferences may be held at times convenient for an employed parent outside the school day. This allows the

classroom teacher to be more readily available than in the past when staffings were routinely scheduled during the time of a teacher's full responsibility for a class.

2. If a conference is scheduled during the school day, the student's major teacher(s) must be present — which may be interpreted to mean that provisions must be made to relieve the teacher of classroom responsibilities to allow parents access to the teacher's report on the student's status.

3. The provision that no single test or evaluation procedure can be the basis for decision ensures a broader base of information to be considered, rendering the teacher's objective records of social and task behaviors as critical as the results of an individual IQ measure (which has sometimes dominated decisions at staffing conferences in the past).

Added safeguards for parent and student rights, therefore, enhance the staffing conference as a forum for exchange of information by a group of specialists speaking from different but equally valid points of view. The teacher—if he or she is to be a full partner in developing the individualized education program—must (a) interpret the reports of fellow professionals with adequate understanding, (b) resolve any conflicts between his or her findings and those of fellow professionals, and (c) maintain a team approach.

INTERPRETATION OF REPORTS

Since parents have access to all records on the student, and because raw data such as test scores may be subject to misinterpretation by untrained persons, a comprehensive written report of each evaluation should be part of the permanent record. The teacher's task in interpreting a written report is less difficult than interpreting an oral report, since the teacher can go back over the written document to check for any inconsistencies or statements requiring clarification. However, oral and written reports contain the same types of statements, and they require the same critical interpretation by a teacher who wishes to make the best use of test results to plan instruction.

Regardless of whether it is delivered in oral or written form, a report of findings by a fellow professional always contains three types of statements—Information, Inferences, and Judgments. This is the case for medical reports as well as psycho-educational reports, but examples from reports by a school psychologist or counselor will illustrate the three types of statements.

Informational Statements

Statements which can be called Information are those which *quantify behavior*. For example, "Mary earned a score of 95% on a page of 20 two-digit subtraction facts," or "Sam earned a full-scale IQ of 95, a verbal IQ of 90, and a performance IQ of 102" are statements which provide Information. Similarly, statements which report test behavior in *objective, observable terms*, such as, "Sally requested examiner aid four times during a 10-minute subtest," or "Bill used his left hand for writing and cutting with scissors" also provide factual data which can be called Information. Reports of the status of a student for an IEP conference usually open with Information statements.

The characteristic which sets Information apart from the other two types of statements is that it is *directly verifiable*. That is, independent scorers and various observers should be able to reach a high level of agreement on statements if they are to be labeled Information statements. If a dispute arises about a statement which quantifies behavior, it should be easily resolved by reference to test record forms or a videotape of the testing session. It is possible for Information to be inaccurate, as when an examiner uses the wrong table to translate raw scores to standard scores, but accurate information is not truly disputable, since it is subject to objective verification. *Information statements are factual*, providing the basis for Inferences and Judgments.

Inferential Statements

An inference is a statement made about the unknown on the basis of what is known. For example, "Jill's writing is handicapped by a developmental lag in visual-motor skills" is an inference drawn from the Information that Jill scored consistently three years below her chronological age on two normed measures of pencil-and-paper copying tasks. *The Inference is an interpretation of the factual data,* and it attempts to integrate two or more test results into a general statement which could be documented by several Information statements. One cannot say that the Inference is absolutely accurate, since Jill's writing also could be influenced by undiagnosed motivational factors, but the Inference is acceptable if it is *based upon a reasonable and economical interpretation of the available test data.*

When disputes arise about Inferences, independent interpreters of the data may not reach a high degree of agreement. Inferences are not directly verifiable through access to observations, since they are abstractions from the data. Nevertheless, Inferences are *subject to documentation by the massing of behavioral indicators.* For example, two Inferences — "Jane demonstrated negative behavior throughout the test," and "Jane lacks self-confidence when faced with an unfamiliar task"— could both be based upon the same observation, that Jane did not attempt 8 of 10 subtest items in one test. The Inference determined to be the more accurate abstraction is the one which can be supported by the weight of the evidence. That is, one must go to the test behavior exhibited by Jane throughout the testing session to examine clusters of behavior which support negativism and those which support lack of self-confidence.

Judgmental Statements

A Judgment is *a statement about action to be taken or about the classification into which a given set of data might fit* — for example, "Joe is appropriate for placement in an EMR classroom," or "Sara demonstrates severe learning disabilities requiring small-group or one-to-one instruction." Statements which may be called Judgments are those which involve comparison of Information and Inferences against a set of criteria, resulting in a decision which is usually expressed in terms of a recommendation. Judgments may be stated by each participant in the staffing conference, and a group Judgment for a specific placement or course of action will serve as a guide for the individualized program.

Judgments are not directly verifiable by observations, but documentation for Judgments is amassed by means of supporting Inferences and Information. Since Judgments are twice removed from factual data, they are subject to greater opportunity for error. Also, since Judgments serve as the basis for the student's program, any error at this level has far-reaching implications for the student and the parents. If Judgments are soundly based upon Inferences, which are in turn drawn from carefully considered Information, Judgments sometimes can be indisputable. In other cases, data and intepretations could support alternative courses, so that the training and experience of the expert making the decision become critical and professional peers may reasonably disagree with the recommendation.

Interaction of Statements in Reports

Statements at the three levels interact in reports; Judgments are based upon Inferences which are based upon Information. An example of a set of statements presented by a school psychologist illustrates the relationship. The recommendation,

> Bob should be placed in a primary learning disabilities resource room for daily instruction in both reading and mathematics

is a Judgment. This Judgment is based upon the following Inferences:

> Bob demonstrates a language deficit which affects his ability to manipulate symbols; he lacks skills in revisualization, spatial relationships, directionality, and visual sequencing. He has average intellectual potential, but learning is limited by inadequate language and organization of

visual information. Bob also is handicapped by overreliance on teacher aid, and he lacks the independent study and social skills to function effectively in a large group for instruction.

These Inferences are, in turn, based upon Information such as the following:

Bob earned a full-scale IQ of 93, a verbal scale of 80, and a performance scale of 111. Vocabulary and Similarities subtest scores were below the mean of other verbal scores. Bob did not carry out a sequence of two oral directions. Picture Completion and Coding subtests, as well as Bender reproductions, were below the norms for his chronological age and below his mean scores for other performance items. Bob stopped twice during pencil-and-paper tasks to ask for examiner aid; he also requested examiner aid on two of three manual manipulation tasks. When a model was present, visual-motor tasks were completed with greater speed, but rotations and inversions of direction still occurred. When the examiner demonstrated a visual-motor task, Bob asked for a repetition of the demonstration, then carried it out in an order the reverse of the model.

When a Judgment is thus supported by detailed Inferences and Information, the teacher is able to determine whether the Judgment is documented. But in a staffing conference the recommendations of experts who evaluated a student are sometimes presented very briefly and without documenting Inferences or Information. Every member of the team must feel free to request documentation for any recommendation.

Even when the examiner attempts to present all relevant information from the testing, however, some difficulties may arise in interpreting each type of statement.

Problems in Interpretation of Statements

At the Information level, the major difficulty for many teachers is that they lack a frame of reference for interpretation of test scores. Unless they have had psychometric training, teachers have only a limited background in the technical considerations surrounding test interpretation. For example, if the teacher is not familiar with the concept of the standard error of measurement (which is a statistic supplied by the test publisher to describe the possible variations in scores of a single individual if he or she took the test a number of times or took alternate forms of the test), the teacher may interpret a test score as a discrete point rather than as a range with a band of probable inaccuracy on either side of the obtained score.

The teacher who will be expected to translate test scores into instructional plans must not take a score too literally but must recognize that it represents a good estimate of the true score. To prepare for sound interpretation of the results of standardized testing, a teacher also should know where to locate information on validity and reliability of specific tests, and should be able to compare the characteristics of the tested student against those of the normative sample for the tests being used by members of the team.

At the level of Inferences, the primary danger is that an inference may be mistaken for factual data. Many examiners have difficulty in stating facts instead of their own interpretations of the facts. A statement such as, "Sue became angry when she could not assemble the fourth block design" is an Inference. The Information statement would read, "Sue worked on the fourth block design for 30 seconds without reproducing it; she then destroyed her attempt by overturning the blocks." An examiner must possess considerable skill and a great deal of self-discipline to report observations as opposed to interpretations of observations.

When reading or listening to a report, a teacher should keep specific questions in mind: Is that *observable,* or would the examiner have to go beyond observation to make that statement? Is that *behavior,* or has the statement gone beyond behavior to report feeling state or attitude of the student? Words which are likely to describe observable behavior are those which involve actions, such as, "Sue pointed to correct items rather than naming them" or "Sue kicked the chair leg repeatedly," as opposed to, "Sue did not know the labels for common household items" or "Sue was tense," which are Inferences.

At the level of Judgments, the major problem may be a tendency to identify the student according to the label which has been applied. An expert's emphasis upon a youngster's intellectual functioning, motor abilities, or hearing may lead him or her to speak of the student as "mentally retarded," "spastic," or "deaf" rather than as a *person* who has many characteristics including slow learning, inability to control movements, or hearing impairment.

Because the attachment of labels can lead to faulty thinking, a teacher must be alert to the effect of such labels on his or her behavior. The teacher would not be likely to overlook the social consequences if a student with protruding ears were to be called "jug-eared" or if a student who was very small should be called "undersized" as an identifying label. Such labels would disregard the many other attributes of the students in question by focusing on one characteristic to the exclusion of others. In the same way, a label such as "emotionally disturbed" or "legally blind" describes only one of the ways of looking at a youngster—a way which is useful only for funding or administrative purposes, and which does not describe the *person*.

RESOLUTION OF DISCREPANCIES

Apparent discrepancies which occur in the status reports of members of the professional team can cause considerable concern to a teacher. Such discrepancies can be the result of differences between the teacher's view of a student and the picture presented by another examiner. Or gaps can occur within the report of a single examiner if statements appear to go beyond or to contradict the scores.

Differences Between Teacher's and Examiner's Views

A teacher on occasion may decide to dismiss test scores reported by another examiner because the scores do not agree with the teacher's own experience with that student. The teacher may have the impression, for example, that Bob's vocabulary is more than adequate in the classroom, and may want to dismiss a test score which indicates that vocabulary is far below age norms.

Although a teacher should recognize the limitations of test scores, he or she is not free to disregard them. If an examiner considers the test valid, the scores must be accepted as one portion of the Information gathered about the student. No single score is interpreted by itself, of course, but it may not be dismissed because it doesn't fit a preconceived pattern. An examiner's statement that Bob is far below average in verbal problem solving may be well documented despite the teacher's own observation that Bob is highly verbal and the first to raise his hand to answer a question. Standardized testing can reveal just such a hidden deficit, and the teacher is wise to remain open to new data from test scores.

In general, the teacher is well advised not to question scores which are *higher* than those predicted from the student's classroom performance. If standardized procedures were followed, it is not possible for a student to perform better than the level of which he is capable; if scores are higher in individual testing than in the classroom, factors other than ability level should be questioned. But if scores are *lower* in a test situation than the teacher would have predicted from classroom performance, they should be checked, since a student can perform at considerably less than optimal level if anxious or unsure of directions. The teacher is responsible for making sure that decisions are not based upon questionable test data.

A teacher may be able to raise the question of the discrepancy in several ways. If an examiner whose report preceded the teacher's own report offered some questionable scores, for example, the teacher may simply remain silent until his or her report is offered, at which time the teacher should point out that his or her results differ from those reported earlier. If the teacher's report has already been presented, the teacher should wait until all the reports have been completed, then raise the question of the discrepancy before any decisions are made. The teacher might say, for example, "Your report of Bob's verbal IQ places him lower than I would estimate from his work in class. Let me give you some examples of what he has done in class to see if they fit with the scores he earned."

The teacher need not accept the score without investigating how it was earned. It is appropriate to ask to see the individual test items. Sometimes the items for a standardized math test, for example, clearly are different enough from those in the classroom text to account for the discrepancy. Or perhaps the method of presentation of items is different. An arithmetic subtest presented orally may be scored lower than similar items presented on paper since task demands are different. A teacher should approach the apparent discrepancy with the point of view that it can be resolved; for example, "Your report of Ann's arithmetic abilities is different from what I've found in the classroom. May I see some examples of the items you presented to see if I can account for the difference?" Such a query fulfills the teacher's obligation to raise the question of an apparent discrepancy, but does not place the other examiner on the defensive.

If examination of test items does not provide an explanation, sometimes the student's task behavior during testing can offer a clue. The teacher may find that descriptions of task behavior are different from those of the student he or she knows. This can happen because teacher and examiner view the student under different conditions. The teacher usually sees the student in a group, doing academic work, and in familiar surroundings. The fifth-grade teacher is concerned primarily with the way in which the student fits into classroom groupings, and notes whether the youngster is developmentally similar to other fifth graders. The examiner sees the student on a one-to-one basis, performing unfamiliar, nonacademic tasks, under timing and stress, working with a comparative stranger. The examiner has been trained to observe subtle differences between individuals which become apparent under standardized presentation.

If the examiner describes the student differently from the way the teacher sees the student, this does not mean that the examiner's observations are to be dismissed. As long as the statements cover observable behavior, the teacher cannot take exception to the task behavior which is reported. The student may not appear that way in the classroom, but the teacher must accept the reality that the student behaved that way in the testing situation. If Joe guessed impulsively in response to verbal items on testing, but typically deliberates before answering a question in class, the teacher should point out the difference in behavior.

The teacher should also use that difference to raise questions about implications for the individualized education program. If a student's task behavior was more efficient or more productive in the testing situation, the teacher should raise the question of whether the pupil needs one-to-one tutoring by a peer or aide; whether he or she requires more variety in tasks rather than the limitation to texts and workbooks; whether the teacher's own or the group's interaction with the student may be less than ideal in the classroom. If the student's task behavior in the testing situation was disorganized in contrast to the classroom, the teacher should ask what implications this has for the pupil's ability to cope with a different volunteer aide every day, with new instructional materials, and with changes in daily routine. If the examiner's observations are accepted and analyzed, the teacher is likely to learn a great deal about the student which will help in planning the program.

Discrepancies within a Report

Some inferences may appear to be stronger than the evidence of scores and test behavior in the report would warrant. The usual explanation for such an occurrence is that the examiner had access to data which were compiled by someone else. Sometimes a student has had prior school district testing which the classroom teacher has not seen. In other cases, a learner may have been evaluated at a community clinic without the teacher's knowledge. Since a good examiner will draw Inferences from all available data, he or she would be wrong to disregard prior testing which is relevant to the current examination. But if such earlier test results are not mentioned in the report, a teacher may discover apparent discrepancies between the data reported and the Inferences drawn from the data. If that happens, a teacher might ask, "Have you reported all the scores on which your statements are based?'

In other cases, Inferences may appear to contradict the reported scores. An examiner may say, for example, that visual-motor skills are well within normal limits; yet the teacher notes that three of five performance scores were far below the mean for other subtests. Two possible explanations could account for such a discrepancy:

1. The basis for inferring strengths might be the *quality* rather than the *quantity* of the responses. A student who misses easy items but responds correctly to much more difficult items will be penalized in scoring, but the level of the accurate responses will indicate ability on the dimension being measured. The examiner's statement might then be based upon the quality of the individual responses rather than the overall score on the subtest.

2. The examiner's consideration of test behavior or situational problems during testing may provide another explanation. The examiner may have noted, for example, that the student didn't look at the model, overdeliberated, or waited for examiner aid, losing points for wasted time. If the examiner is satisfied that the items which were completed demonstrated adequate skills, the lowered score can be explained by the inappropriate test behavior and factors other than basic visual-motor skills.

MAINTENANCE OF THE TEAM APPROACH

When differing views regarding a student must be reconciled, each person who has evaluated the student must feel absolutely comfortable in raising questions. When several individuals share equal responsibility for development of an individualized education program, test findings and recommendations from each professional person must be considered as carrying equal weight in the deliberations which lead to decisions. The regular classroom teacher, who has not always been a member of a team serving the special needs of the exceptional student, must adjust his or her own view of the teacher's role in order to be a full partner. Placing this role into perspective may involve adopting a specific orientation to testing as part of the assessment process, respecting one's own professional expertise as well as that of colleagues, assuming a position as student advocate, and developing a set of realistic expectations for the team.

Acceptance of the Psychometric Orientation

In referring a student for testing, a teacher makes certain commitments to the psychometric orientation. The teacher must adjust his or her thinking toward the comparison of a student with other youngsters of the same chronological age and grade level. This type of comparison is considered inappropriate by some teachers who prefer to judge a student against absolute criteria rather than norms. Although informal criterion-referenced assessment is entirely appropriate for purposes of programming in a classroom, decisions regarding placement in a special classroom or delivery of special services programs require the documentation offered by standardized tests. Norm-referenced tests cannot predict how a student will respond to an individualized program, but they can offer some insight into capabilities as measured against numbers of youngsters in the standardization sample, so that individual strengths, weaknesses, and general characteristics can emerge from such a comparison.

Willingness to accept the quantification of behavior which is provided by standardized, norm-referenced tests is part of the agreement between the teacher and the many support persons who may be asked to participate in the assessment of a given student. Once the psychometric approach has been taken, test scores cannot be disregarded as long as the examiner considers them valid. A teacher is not justified in permitting subjective appraisal of the student to supersede test data provided by other

111

experts. Instead, all data collected about a given learner must be considered and reconciled into a set of documented recommendations.

But acceptance of the psychometric approach does not mean disregard for the limitations of tests, nor does it mean that alternatives to testing will not be sought. A teacher who is to participate in staffings in which results of standardized tests will be reported should become acquainted with the aspects of test construction and qualification which will allow interpretation of a test score. The teacher also should consider that willingness to accept the psychometric approach when it is appropriate does not imply that it is always appropriate. Sometimes subjecting a given learner to psychometric evaluation will not be the proper course to take. The teacher who is a member of a team will be free to consult team members about the appropriateness of testing or to formulate the referral question in such a way as to make reservations clear.

Respect for Professional Competence

Only if members of a team view themselves as co-professionals—each with unique but equal skills to offer—can they disagree constructively or come to satisfactory agreement about courses of action. Respect for the expertise of a fellow professional sometimes comes more readily to a teacher than does respect for his or her own expertise. Some teachers may defer to the decisions of a psychologist, for example, out of awe at the mystique of this specialized knowledge which teachers do not have.

Instead, a teacher should recognize the value of his or her own understanding of the learning process, the developmental level of pupils of a given age range, the sequence of skills in subject matter areas, selection and modification of materials, and the day-to-day behavior of a student for whom the teacher has access to unlimited samples of behavior. The teacher's *skills* are different from those of a psychologist or audiologist, but the *contribution* is equal. Women teachers may defer to fellow professionals who are men, because acculturation may have led them to consider the male voice as the voice of authority. Some teachers may defer to colleagues who are older, or to persons in authority over them, such as principals or other administrators. Such orientations are not compatible with the team approach.

At the other extreme, some teachers may consider that they are the only ones who have expertise about students assigned to them. Such teachers may have difficulty accepting the fact that a trained psychologist can learn a great deal about a student from two hours spent administering a well-selected battery of standardized tests. They may dismiss recommendations which are sound because the person who offered them "has never taught 30 children in a class." If detailed procedures suggested by an expert contain one or two items which could not be implemented because of space or materials limitations, a teacher might label the entire package "impractical."

Too many examiners have had the experience of accepting a referral from a teacher, testing, writing a report, and making recommendations, only to learn that the teacher has not implemented any of the suggestions nor requested a conference to discuss any areas of disagreement. Such passive rejection of the work of a fellow professional is seriously damaging to the team and unfair to the student who deserves to have instructional decisions based upon all available professional expertise.

To be regarded as an equal member who is the expert on the student's academic functioning, the teacher might adopt certain guidelines:

1. The teacher never goes beyond the evidence in reporting the youngster's capabilities; speculation has no part in the reports—only observed Information, data-based Inferences, and documented Judgments.

2. The teacher retains flexibility about what he or she is willing to try in terms of interventions recommended by other members of the team, with due consideration for the needs of other students in the classroom.

3. If convinced that an intervention is impractical or inappropriate, the teacher states the case tactfully and offers an alternative.

4. When the teacher agrees to an intervention in the classroom, he or she does so for a specific period of time, with a clear understanding of the time and the person responsible for reevaluation of the intervention, and of the teacher's own role in regard to record maintenance.

5. The teacher limits Judgments to the academic area of expertise, and does not ask fellow professionals to go beyond their areas of competence.

A teacher who considers himself or herself a member of a professional team maintains a high regard for the ethical principles and practices of colleagues. This teacher also maintains a high standard of conduct. He or she recognizes that test scores, task behaviors, and statements about a student's needs are appropriately discussed only with other members of the team or with the student's parents. The teacher guards against verbal publication of a student's status in the teachers' lounge or when conversing with aides, volunteers, or non-professional school staff, and exercises care over the disposition of written records or reports.

Advocacy of Student Welfare

Ethical conduct as a member of a team goes far beyond confidentiality of information. It involves recognition of the responsibility of each member of the team to advocate the student's welfare above any other considerations. Although each member of the team shares equally in this responsibility, the classroom teacher may be in the best position to serve as student advocate, because the teacher usually has the first contact and the most continuous contact with the student. Thus, the teacher is in a position to gain an overview of the student's status which experts testing one facet of the youngster may not have.

Also, the regular classroom teacher, who sees typical, achieving children every day, while expert diagnosticians may see only the youngsters who deviate from norms, is likely to be in the best position to see how a given student is *similar* to others in the classroom rather than ways in which he or she is *different*. This factor allows the teacher to bring a certain authority to statements that the student can function in the regular classroom, and the teacher may be the only member of the team who can accurately assess the prognosis for the youngster in the regular class. This is an awesome responsibility, and one which no teacher will take lightly when decisions about the least restrictive environment are to be made.

The teacher's role as an advocate may take many forms. It certainly means that the teacher will raise questions about any discrepancies between his or her view of the student and that presented by other team members. It may mean taking exception to a recommendation which seems to jeopardize the student's self-concept or social standing with peers. In assuming the position of advocate, the teacher is careful to respect channels of authority and school policies, but maintains a view of the individual youngster through the paperwork involved in the assessment process.

Recognition of Team Limitations

A regular classroom teacher is required to make many decisions in the course of instruction of assigned students. In the case of students who exhibit possible handicapping conditions, specific functions or behaviors which interfere with response to instruction can be identified by referral to diagnostic specialists, who then participate in the decisions which lead to an individualized education program. This process benefits both the teacher and the student.

However, even when a teacher has correctly identified an exceptional youngster, has diagnosed academic status, formulated useful referral questions, and requested assistance from support personnel, one cannot expect that instructional problems will *always* be solved by careful professional evaluation of a student. For stubborn instructional dilemmas, testing by other experts will prove less useful than the teacher's own systematic trial teaching over time to answer questions of materials selection, sequencing of tasks, and pace of instruction.

Furthermore, the best reports by experts on the characteristics of exceptional learners cannot translate recommendations into activities which fit into Mr. Jones' fifth-grade classroom —he is the only one who knows the classroom well enough to do that. Therefore, a teacher cannot expect a school psychologist or a counselor to provide cookbook recommendations covering methods and materials, nor that a medical consultant can anticipate every possible classroom adjustment for a physically handicapped student.

The teacher who is a member of a team maintains realistic expectations of other members of the team and recognizes that there are limitations upon the assistance they will be able to provide as the learner's status is assessed. The availability of diagnostic specialists does not limit the teacher's responsibility for designing classroom instruction. Consultation with the diagnostic team is merely one resource available to the classroom teacher in assuming responsibility in development of the individualized education program. The successful mainstreaming teacher is one who recognizes the teacher's own ultimate responsibility for interpreting diagnostic findings into appropriate instructional practices in the regular classroom.